THE RELIGIONS AND HIDDEN CULTS OF INDIA

THE RELIGIONS AND HIDDEN CULTS OF INDIA

GEORGE MACMUNN

GYAN

Published by

Gyan Publishing House
5, Ansari Road
Daryaganj, New Delhi-110002
Phone: 011-47034999, 9811692060
E-mail: books@gyanbooks.com

Distribution Network
gyanbooks.com
India, USA, Canada, UK, Australia

ISBN: 978-93-6780-170-3 (HB)

First Published, 1931

2nd Impression 2024

Printed at: Gyan Press, Delhi.

THE RELIGIONS AND HIDDEN CULTS OF INDIA
Author: GEORGE MACMUNN

THE RELIGIONS AND HIDDEN CULTS OF INDIA

The Great Stone Temples at Ellora
The devoted craftsmanship of Hindu Temples

Frontispiece.

THE RELIGIONS AND HIDDEN CULTS OF INDIA

By LIEUT.-GENERAL

SIR GEORGE MACMUNN

K.C.B., K.C.S.I., D.S.O., *p.s.c.*,

Colonel Commandant The Royal Artillery.

LONDON

SAMPSON LOW, MARSTON & CO., LTD.

INTRODUCTORY NOTE

So many friends and acquaintances have asked me questions of the religions of India and what they really mean, that I have endeavoured to put them in outline, with some slight illustration for the arm-chair reader, who has no time or call for deeper study. Since I have touched on subjects which comprise one of the most extensive bibliographies of the world, I refrain from enumerating even a few of the great works, but for those who would go slightly deeper, I would commend some of the little books of the Society for the Propagation of the Gospel, *Islam* and *Buddhism* in Benn's Sixpenny Series, and the like. A reference to the *Encyclopœdia of Ethics and Religion*, will give plenty of references, while under each heading the *Encyclopœdia Britannica* alone will give more references than any but the scholar dare face.

I have attached a glossary of a few of the terms met with most generally in ordinary references to Indian faiths.

Among others the author is indebted to the Indian Railway Bureau, to the Society for the Propagation of the Gospel to the Indian Archaeological Department (whose photographs are copyright) for permission to reproduce the illustrations in this book.

CONTENTS

ILLUSTRATIONS

MAP

THE RELIGIONS AND HIDDEN CULTS OF INDIA

CHAPTER I

THE MANY WAYS OF HINDUSTAN

THE KEYS OF ALL THE CREEDS—PILGRIMS—THE DRUM OF ISLAM—THE SPRINGFRET—THE FESTIVAL OF FECUNDITY—THE MANY WAYS—THE MULTIPLE RELIGIONS OF INDIA—THE DISCIPLES OF BABA NANAK—THE HIDDEN PATHS.

THE KEYS OF ALL THE CREEDS

"And he said unto me, in the beginning, when the earth was made, before the borders of the world stood, or ever the winds blew,

"Before it thundered and lightened, or ever the foundations of paradise were laid,

"Before the fair flowers were seen, or ever the moveable powers were established, before the innumerable multitude of angels were gathered together,

"Or ever the heights of the air were lifted up, before the measures of the firmamant were named, or ever the chimneys in Sion were hot,

"And ere the present years were sought out, or ever the inventions of them that now sin were turned, before they were sealed that have gathered faith for a treasure:

"Then did I consider these things, and they were all made through me alone, and through none other: by me also shall they be ended and none other."—II. ESDRAS vi, 1–6.

Amid the great religions of the East, that stood 'before the present years were sought out', are those whose origins are lost in the mists of time, and which even to this day throw up more signs of the stress and strain, of the springs and wells of life, and of the working of the peoples, than is normal in the more placid unheeding West.

Before endeavouring to see them even in outline, let us try and stir our imaginings with some vignetted scenes, the pilgrims in their quest of the 'Way', the fierce Moslem priest on the frontier seeking paradise on the bayonet's point, and the women in the temples knowing that a soul cannot return to the world to work out release unless they play their part.

Pilgrims

"Peace on the uttermost borders
Strength on a road untold."

"*Challo Bhayan! Challo!*" "Hurry brothers, hurry!" and the eager jostling crowd cast their eyes to the snows above, and jingled and tramped along the mountain paths. The peasants and even the traders had left their shacks and their booths and had come tramping up from the plains of India, through the passes and over the snows of the outer Himalaya. Old and young, men and matrons, lads and maidens, cowherds and farmers, fishers and spearmen, ascetic and *faqir*, parents and children. "*Un qui marche, un qui tette, un qui vient*", they streamed out of the Holy city. From Baramullah they crowded, over the Pir through Shapiyon, down the valley from Verinag, eager to ease the heartache by the cool tarn and the sacred shrine amid the glaciers on Holy Haramukh. And as they pressed, these tens of thousands of Hindus, the world of Islam in the villages watched and wondered, cursing in their hearts the misbegotten idolators. Far away into the plains of the Happy Valley tailed the crowds that surged from the Punjab and from Hindustan, past the ruined Pandav temples, past the almond orchards, past the mosques of Allah, who shared worshippers with no partner Gods, out on the *karewa* plateau by the dog-rose, the wild thyme, and the iris blooming in the grave-yards.

> "Come brothers, come! for the snow are far,
> Come brothers, come! to the healing shrine,
> Come brothers, come! for the peace that endures."

The great pilgrimage, the yearly pilgrimage to Haramukh in Kashmir was in full force, and all the yearning for release and peace on a road untold, that lies at the bottom of the heart of man and woman, but most especially man, seemed released in that hurrying crowd, that had been marching for days, or driving by the cart road in bullock wagon and pony cart.

Many there were who dropped by the road way, and here and there a family stepped aside that the mother might give birth behind the blanket screen to the '*un qui vient*': a few hours and she with her shouldered babe would be tramping on again. Past pine and fir and spruce, past *cedar deodaris*, and out of the forest to the scattered silver birch, the juniper scrub and the bilberry, past the wayside cairn that some pious Moslem may have built, on to the tarn and the deep black pool and the bubbling well and the grey stone shrine. There would be the promised peace, and the balm.

And down on the road where the press lay heaviest an aged Jesuit, in white soutain and black scull-cap moved and worked. Here a word and there a hand, and in his hand the keys of all the creeds, while far above a poised eagle scanned the depth.

The Drum of Islam

"And ye reap a bloody harvest with the sickle of the Lord."

"*Ya Allah! Ya Allah! Allah Ho Akbar!*" "God is all-mighty!" The Hadeedah mullah, tall and gaunt with a ragged beard set on his thin polemical chin, which shone out in silhouette against the wood-fires, strode into the assembly followed by the *shahids*, the witnesses to the Faith. Rub-a-dub! Rub-a-dub! went the tomtoms, a stirring roll with a kick to it, just like the drums of the Guards as they leave St. James's. Rub-a-dub, Rub-a-dub, Rub-dub-a-dub-dub-dub! The clansmen rose and shouted the *Kalima of Islam*. "*La Illah ha, il·Illah ho!*" ("There is no God but Allah"), and then back from the rocks came the answer, "*Wa Muhammad Rasul il Illah*" ("And Muhammad is his prophet").

A revivalist meeting was in progress in Waziristan, not a doubt of it. The sun had gone to its setting behind the great peak of Shuidar, and the cool breeze of evening whistled through the deodars, those deodars that foolish tribesmen are fast destroying, cedars which like their kinsmen of Lebanon long that the sound of the feller should cease.

The Hadeedah mullah lived in a grotto by the Tangdarra Pass high up on the road to Ghuzni, just within the line on the paper map which separated nominal Afghanistan from nominal India, nominal because neither King of Kabul nor Emperor of India could not, or dared not, administer the devil hills through which the map-made line was traced. Amanullah of Kabul had made his useless faithless invasion of India, afraid of his own army, and anxious to give it something to do. The tribes on the British border had harried and shot and raided the peaceful Indian cultivators of the Indus valley, during the World War, and when Amanullah made the venture that brought his downfall in its train, the eager frontiersmen had hurried in his wake . . . hurried to the sack of India.

Amanullah had been kicked back whence he came, by the half demobilized Indo-British army, but the peace of the border so grievously upset was now to heal. To help civilize the clansmen and the better to protect the plains folk, the British had pushed motor roads and established fresh frontier posts.

The Hadeedah mullah and the more fanatical of his neighbours were aggrieved thereat. Moreover, there had been a falling off of revenue at the shrine. A stimulant with a big 'S' was required . . . a revival of Islam that would lead the clansmen straight on to the British bayonets, and overwhelm them were they stood guard.

So the clans of Central Waziristan were assembled in a green grass basin and cup in the hills, with the cliffs of their cave-dwellings round, and the Mullah and his *Shahids* were beating like mad on the drum ecclesiastic. "Heaven for all and Glory for those who bleed," and even the women in the shadows behind the camp fires that glowed as twilight fell, beat their lips with their hands, *Lu! Lu! Lu!*

The mullah had sat long in his mountain-top gleaning the news of the world, from the passing caravans and biting his nails in idleness. He was a *Sayad*, that is to say, a descendant of the Prophet, of the holy tribe of the Qoreish, to which the Prophet had belonged. His face was an Arab face, long and somewhat drawn, with a large thin nose and a cleft chin, tight closed lips, and shaggy eyebrows from which gleamed two fierce dark eyes. All the fire and all the zeal which had carried Islam at the point of the sword over a large portion of the civilized Eastern world, and even through Spain into France, shone in those zealot eyes.

Now had an opportunity come. The British had insisted on driving a devil road for their fire carriages, right through Waziristan. This was a horror and an outrage, which all the tribes felt, and in their trouble turned to religion, or at any rate, listened to the Hadeedah mullah, and the surge and thunder of the drum ecclesiastic. Once again the cry that the Faith was in danger, fell on responsive ears.

The flicker of the camp fires in the ring showed rows of tribal chiefs, and their followers seated on the ground, and behind them in their dark garments the dour unwanted tribal women, that the wounded know to dread.

Into the gathering strode the *mullah* followed by his disciples and drums. Halting by a big grey stone on the grass in the centre, he boomed out the sonorous Arabic greeting "*As Salaam aleikum!*" ("Peace be with you!"), and back came the answer from the gathering, "*Wa aleikum Salaam!*" ("And peace be with you too!"). And he once again before speaking in their own tongue the stately Arabic "*B'ism Illah, ur rahman o ulkarim*" ("In the name of God, the All-Merciful and All-compassionate"), and then he broke into the Pushto of that part of the Frontier. "How had they fallen away from their high estate! How had the infidel come to build roads and forts! How was it that their *purdah*, the curtain of their life was lifted for ever! How was it that their name was a jest and a by-word among the women even all the border round! How had the old men stood it! Were they afraid?

Fie! *Fie!* Greybeards must die! Cursed be they who held the young men back!

"You are only fit for slaves. Will I lead you! I will not. When I face British cannon I want better hearts at my back. What! You protest you will follow where I led! Then I will trust you once more. I have a charm! I will bless you; those who I bless will bear a charmed life, no English bullet can touch them. Only believe and you are immune! If any one falls by your side he is a doubter, and a coward! Glory for all! and Heaven for those who bleed has been the rule. But I say to you 'Glory for all, and immunity for those who believe! *Ya Allah! Ya Allah!*'"

And the drums rolled once again, with that throb and kick, which the experienced drummer produces with his palms and the pad of his fingers. The spirit took hold, like the roar of a forest fire. "*Ya Allah! Ya Allah!*" The clansmen leapt to their feet, and waved their swords and rifles. "Lead us, Holy Mullah! Lead Us!" and again the women shouted, calling, *Lu Lu Lu!* and the blood leapt in the listeners' hearts.

Two hours before the dawn, long silent strings of men came streaming down the course of the Tawi Zam, their shoes in their hands to the cover of a long low ridge whence three ravines led to the British post which would bring them unseen to within three hundred yards of the perimeter. It was true that three hundred yards of open fire-swept sward remained, but had not the Holy Mullah promised immunity! Every lad knew that, and enthusiasm carefully stimulated by the *shahids* surged within their breasts. Seventeen green standards were there, with fifty swordsmen to each, and a party of men, grown old in the

British service, were to close in on the southern face and keep up a well-aimed rifle fire, while on the northern face, the swordsmen crept up the ravines. The sniping would keep the English alert on the north side, till the swordsmen crept quite near. The attack must not take place till near dawn so that any martyr might see the sun rise if the mullah's blessing failed them.

But the British had a misbegotten of habit of standing to arms an hour before dawn and though the gathering clans knew it not, four hundred British and Indian soldiers leaned on their rifles the perimeter round. Bang! Bang! Two rifle shots rang out in the crisp cool dawn air, followed by a couple more. The Commandant of the garrison hurried to his command post. As he did so the throb of a drum rolled from the same direction as the shots. This time a ragged volley followed. "Looks as if we were for it, for a change!" was his only comment. The troops gripped their rifles tighter, and reserve platoons stiffened.

The firing on the one side grew fiercer, and on the other, out of the haze and the smoke of the litter burning in the ravines, rose the throb of more drums, Rub-a-dub! Rub-a-dub! Rub-dub! and out of the ravines appeared scurrying figures. "*Ya Allah! Ya Allah!*" But it was three hundred yards to bear down in the open against a post whose routine was readiness. The troops started firing steadily as the fierce cries of the *shahids* burst forth, and the banners could be seen in the glowing light. The firing on the north side increased, and was now being steadily replied to. Cr . . . rack went the Maxim guns, and huddled lumps of grey were dotting the sward.

"*Ya Allah!*" came the cries from the rushing tribesmen, and the standards crept to the head of the ravine, and then were carried forward as the drums took up the infection.

"On! On! Never mind the grey huddled heaps of the doubters, they have got their deserts. You are immune! On to the parapets where the infidels await your swords. Glory for all, and Heaven for those who bleed!"

The mullah on his hillock by his great green standard, saw his lads afalling, and heard the swift crack of the defenders' bullets on the rocks. The glare of a star shell from the mountain guns showed him a gleam of steel, and huddled little heaps of his heroes. "Was he wrong? Was his charm a failure? Had he not the blessing of Allah, on his enterprise of faith and glory? Oh! Surely. There is no God but Allah! There is no prophet but Muhammad!"

The fierce old man seized his standard himself and girded up his loins, and ran with his *shahids* and drummers following. How they throbbed and how the bullets sang and cracked on the rocks around. There! They are in! Hear the fierce shouts. *Din! Din! Fatteh Muhammad!* ("The Faith! The Faith! Victory to the Prophet!").

Alas, the race is not always to the swift nor victory to the enthusiasms. The reserve platoons had brought their bayonets to the charge with a vicious snap of the rifle sling, and were clearing out those few who had penetrated the perimeter, the clansmen were scuttling back to the ravines. Crash fell the Hadeedah mullah with a bullet through his lungs, and, as he lay adying, he could see willing hands roll back a spiked gate-barrier and a score of lancers canter forth. Blowing bubbles of blood and froth, his dimming eye could see his lads laying silent on the sward, and could hear the cries of the pursuing troopers. "*Allah ho Akhbar! Fatteh Muhammad!*" and that fierce spirit was required of him.

The Springfret

"The organs of birth and the circlet of bones,
and the loose loves carved on the temple stones"—

Over the lake and along the canal had come the boats, full of women swathed in veils, silent save for the muffled strokes of the boatmen at the paddles and the mutter of the waters under the prows. Women were flocking to the great female festival of Spring and fecundity, the world was awakening from its winter and since man's soul may go from human to beast, and from beast to plant in working out his destiny and expiating his *karma*, all that means life is sacred and pregnant. The women went to worship *en masse* at the fount of fertility. By water and by road in little curtained bullock carts, the crowd grew and grew. The *chajna*, the clatter of women's tongues was still, and the occasion solemn beyond description.

In the temple, hundreds of women sat packed in the darkness, before the huge mass of an image carved in black basalt, before which now and again into a great brass basket of embers a priest threw something that made the fire leap high in lapping, sensuous flames, lighting up for a moment the carvings on the rock, the outline of the image, the glistening drops that shone on its head from some drip above, and the loose loves carved on the stones. A chaunt that was almost a dirge came from the dark recesses, and now and again a drum throbbed, throbbed to the urge for life and fecundity that was slowly rising in the psychology of that great mass of worshippers. Siva, Mahadeo, the Great God, the god of life and death,

A Mukhi-Linga (many faced linga) of the more conventional type
With Female Emblem at Top. (S. India)

the god of worldlings, of mothers in childbirth, of merry-makers on their rounds each to each and all to all. Now high, now low, rose and fell the chaunt and the multitude bowed in unison, more insistent grew the drums and more expressive of that desire that sees to it that the world shall continue. Man must hurry through his carnal lives, so that a soul may work up its way to salvation, or fall to hell and start again, on the slippery path of re-incarnation. Again the flames leapt and a conch braved, and the chaunt now dwelt on the duty of every woman to conceive in joy and people the world, and the mass of bowed figures seemed to emanate response. Through the gloom, the eyes of those who dared to look could see the scenes and emblems and allegories of fertility carved on the dim reeking walls of stone.

"I am the God of the sensuous fire,
That moulds all nature in form divine,
The symbols of death and of man's desire,
The springs of change in the world are mine."

Outside, out from the gloom and the scent of the incense of sandal and champak and samphire, out from the oppression of a thousand throbbing as one, a girl supported by an elder woman sobbed and gasped, half carried, half dragged, through a wicket to cool green turf on the waters bank hard by. As the girl collapsed on the grass, came up a figure in pale safron dress, a figure with a face that bore the marks of peace on a road untold, even the Peace of God which passeth all understanding. The Swami Sri Ananda paused and passed his hand in front of the maid.

"Daughters, what seek ye here?"

"We seek coolth and rest. My daughter-in-law is overcome in the temple. Baba! I want quiet and rest for her."

"Rest and quiet she shall have and the blessing of Indra. See," and he drew them, the younger now somewhat recovered, to a shrine hard by. "See! all is cool and peaceful. See the brow of Indra. Peace! Peace on a road untold."

> "And the burden of thought and the travail of care,
> Weigh down the soul in its wandering flight."

"All are gone in the dreamless night." And the image of Indra smiled as the Swami smiled, free of all care and full of all confidence.

"And the temple whence we have come?" and as she spoke the faint throb of a drum in the interior seemed to come through the mulberry grove, the pale sheen of the spring dress of the trees and the soft soughing of the wind in the boughs, seemed an answer.

"Temples and gods, daughter, temples and gods? One in all and all in one. There are gods no more, but their spells remain."

> "Ye have courted them vainly with passion and prayer,
> Ye shall live by knowledge and peace and love."

The Many Ways

The three scenes from India life just presented, should serve to focus our attention on all the urge of religious feelings of one kind and another, that lie beneath the veil of everyday life in the East . . . the craving for something beyond man's ken, in the great contentment of Hinduism and the fierce urge of wilder Islam.

In sensing the general world-interest that current affairs have aroused in matters Indian since 1929, it is almost commonplace to remark that the land is as big as Europe less Russia, that it contains 350,000,000 souls, that it has many widely divergent races, over two hundred different languages, and many different religions. All the world knows these points, yet fails to conceive their significance. Nor does it seem to be able to attach due weight to the fact that since the days of our Norman Conquest, India has been ruled by invaders from the North, or that with one short exception, its dynasties have been Turks or Tartars, a word by the way that should be written Tatar, and pronounced like a postman's knock. The fact that Great Britain has woven in a remarkable manner, in the last hundred and fifty years, the thousand and one pieces into which the Mogul Empire had broken, into one peaceful and prosperous whole, seems also to be little realized in the wave of misunderstanding in which half the world prefers to bathe.

Such points, however, are outside the purpose of this book, to expound, which rather aims at showing in outline for those who would have a bowing acquaintance therewith, the divergent religions, their origins, and the many strange cults which, springing therefrom, tend to countless variation and immense heights of good and depths of evil. Between the almost Christ-like teaching of the Bhakti cult of Salvation that Hindu philosophy has evolved, to the lowest depths of left-handed Saktism lies a gamut of religious thought and use that is wrapt in mystery. From the saintly figure of a Bhodi-satva amid the transfrontier ruins of ancient Ghandara to the thrice obscene inter-twining of *yoni* and *linga* in a Madras temple, there is an extreme range of thought and allegory, and all that is good and evil and pitiful in the human mind.

From the Jain and Buddhists of the south to the fierce monotheism of Islam, and the ancient fire-worship of the Parsees, there is an astounding way to go. In hill and jungle tracts, where the aboriginal tribes still worship snake and devil, Christianity brings its message, even from ancient Nestorian days and the legend of St. Thomas, to the Salvation Army taming the wildest and finding a soul where soul could hardly be.

Temple prostitutes and hermits in their cell shelter under the umbrella of Hinduism—

> "The organs of birth and the circlet of bones
> and the loose loves carved on the temple stones"—

are side by side with the swastika and emblems of purity and eternity. Even the seal of David jostles the Crescent and the lotus, for ancient Jewish settlements black and white shelter in the land, almost since time was, and on the walls of the tomb of the Moslem saint Chisti at Fatehpur Sikri, the city of Akbar the Great, it is written:

> "And Jesus said, the world is a bridge
> You must not build on it."

So new and yet so like!

These religions and cults and their hidden ways have been aptly referred to by Rudyard Kipling in the "The Mother Lodge".

> "Muhammad God and Siva changing piquets all the while."

and if we would learn of the inner cults one must know enough of the main religions of India in their everyday purpose to be qualified to watch the guard-mounting.

An Attendant at the Shrine of the Moslem Saint Chisti
Stately Islam

The Multiple Religions of India

The religions of India might almost be called legion, so diverse are the cults of the more untutored tribes, but eight great faiths hold the field. Given in their date of origin or arrival they may be marshalled as follows:

Hinduism
Jainism
Buddhism
Judaism
Christianity
Islam
Sikhism

the eighth is the religion of the Parsees, the ancient cult of Zarathrusthra whom we call Zoroaster, which however is outside India, in that no Indians profess it, and which came as a sojourner when Islam thrust the fire-worshippers or Parsis (which is only another form of the word Persians), out from their ancient land. Aryans themselves, their religion as old as Hinduism, but has travelled so far in thought, when the Aryans of Iran separated from the Aryans who came to India, that they have few points in common and neither make nor lose proselytes except so far as now and again they become Christians. Hinduism which began with the simplest faiths of pastoral people in the forces of nature and the spirit behind them, had developed many hundred years before Christ into the most complete and complex belief that the world has yet seen.

By the sixth century B.C. the subtle Aryan brain had developed this religion so complicated and so ornate, and withal so devoid of a Way of Life that there arose two entirely separate though analagous religious movements of simplicity and purity, viz., those taught by Mahavira the Jinna, which men call Jain, and by Prince Gautama the Buddha. The one was to cut no great mark yet to fall among the wealthy who could do it material honour, the latter to pass through many stages, to become for centuries the philosophy of India and eventually to grow to be a religion and embrace half the East.

As the years rolled on Buddhism spreads with the coming of the Tartar to the Indus, as the religion of China and Central Asia, but loses after a predominance of close on a thousand years, its hold of India, as the clever Brahmin brain re-asserts supremacy. Hardly has it done so when the faith of the Prophet, the great monotheistic faith of Islam 'The Submission', i.e. submission to the will of God, sweeps the near and middle East. It comes to the mouths of the Indus from the city of Sinbad the Sailor, the Bussorah and Basra of our day, in the eighth century, but comes no farther. It is lapping round the mountains of Central Asia, surging into the source of the Oxus and the gorges of the Hindu Kush, but does not come into India again till it rushes with irresistible force on the sword points of invading races from out the Mountains of Solomon, over the Indus and far into Hindustan, almost as the Normans swarmed into Britain. When it comes, it brings the martyrs death, Islam or the sword, but it also brings that which had swung India towards Buddhism a thousand years and more before. It brought to the sensuous and ineffective Hindu theology an entirely new viewpoint, a single God, the God of Abraham and Isaac and Jacob, with a new Prophet, powerful to save, before whom all men and all races were equal. The Moslem, the practicer of Islam 'The Submission', need be of no twice-born race. The aboriginal and the outcaste on whom the twice-born spat, found himself being told that he too had a place in this world and the next. Just as Christianity had brought in the near East, hope and status to all who were desolate or oppressed, so came Islam to India. While hundreds of thousands accepted the faith at the sword's point, as many more enlisted under the banner of the Prophet because it gave them freedom and uplift and a goal that man could attain, a goal too, to which had some co-relation with human desires.

The faith moreover appealed not only to the outcaste inferior tribes of the old enslavement, but to the northern Rajput races, who in the Punjab, and more especially in what we now call the Frontier hills, became enthusiastic supporters of the teaching of the Prophet and so have they remained to this day. The Moslems thus flocked down, and with their zealous new converts tore down the ornate Hindu temples, and slew hundred of thousands of those who would not listen. To this day down the Jumma and Ganges stand the ruins of the Hindu temples destroyed by Mahmud of Ghuzni the *Butshikan* or idol breaker. The famous temples of Somnath in Guzerat were destroyed, the priests slain, the wealth removed to the great centre of Islam, learning and sanctity rising in the Afghan hills at Ghuzni.

Thus came Islam to India, bringing with it in the persons of the fierce northern races, Semite, Tartar, and also Aryan, the domination which was to last from the days of our Norman William to those of the Hanoverian George, and to leave that legacy of ill-will which dormant under a century and a half of British pacification, has burst out under the evil influence of the Western political ballot box. Akbar, the greatest of the great Moguls, strove hard to heal the sore, adopting among other acceptable plans the pleasant method of marrying ninety Hindu ladies of high lineage, and even devising a world religion, which should satisfy all men. But oil and water can never mix, and the hard faith of Islam can never lie with either the popular or the purer forms of Hinduism. The faith of Al Islam is largely of the Orthodox order, though the Shiahs, the sect of the great schism, are represented in India, as well as certain peculiar bodies under the banner of the Prophet which, will be outlined later.

Despite the foolish utterances of Baba Ghandi, Christianity is an old faith in this mighty continent with equal right to spread itself. The ancient Church of Asia which Rome in contempt has called Nestorian, after its leader who outside the Roman Empire came not to Nicea, has flourished in India, from, it is said, A.D. 200. As it stretched all over Persia even to China, that is no wonder, but save in India it went down before Islam, the faith which some say is but the preparer of races not yet fit for Christianity. Nevertheless that Church which has several branches, has flourished in South India and taught of Isa ibn Miriam, for many centuries before ever Muhammad ibn Abdullah ever showed the way of Al Islam.

In 1546 came to India with the Portuguese settlement the famous missionary, St. Francis Xavier, bringing the teaching and message of Christ from the Church of Rome appealing to many peasant souls on the West Coast, and forming an ecclesiastical province which has now its hold all over India, with many a cathedral and school. Further during the last half century, there has been growing up in the south, amid the poor and depressed, as in the days of Rome, a remarkable Christian population, among the outcaste and enslaved races, taught by the various Protestant Missions, who now realize that a United Church is needed which shall not perpetuate the lesser doctrinal differences of the West.

THE DISCIPLES OF BABA NANAK

When Martin Luther was preaching in the Holy Roman Empire there arose in the north of India one Baba Nanak, who taught a simple kindly faith open to all mankind. Incurring the quite needless enmity of the Moslem Government of Delhi it became under Guru Govindh, the tenth teacher in succession from Nanak, to be a fierce militant body, forged on anvils hot with pain, which under a chief was to blossom for the space of one man's life into a ruling race and control a kingdom. This faith was that known as Sikhism, Sikh meaning 'disciple' from the verb '*sikhna*' ('to learn'), and is erroneously, from many aspects, described as an off-shoot of Hinduism. Because Sikhism was favoured by the pick of the manly folk of the Punjab, it was able to gain a reputation far in excess of its numbers, which to this day of all ages and both sexes numbers little over three million souls. The teaching of Baba Nanak would have charmed any kindly philosopher, leading men far from strife, from the fierce practice of Islam and the sensuous impressions of the Hinduism of the by-ways. With Guru Govindh came also the fierce spirit that re-acts to persecution, and the dour simple rules of life that bound the Sikh as soldiers, appealed immensely to the British officer.

Courage, faithfulness, austerity were its principles and its members all adopted the title *Singh*, or 'Lion,' which hitherto the Rajput Aryans had kept strictly to themselves. Though Sikhism was, in theory, open to all, to Moslem and to outcaste, yet inherent prejudice kept the latter out, nor indeed did centuries of oppression tend to breed in the latter the qualities that make a 'singh.' But because a fraternity of scavengers rescued from a Mogul execution dock the crucified body of one of the Gurus, that fraternity was admitted to be 'disciples' of the Sikh brotherhood, receiving the cognomen *mazabi* or 'faithful' which they retain to this day, and are faithful soldiers of His Majesty. But Sikhism, certainly Singhism, is a dour faith, and when times of stress are past ill suited perhaps to the less strenuous life of a pacified East. Thirty years ago, Sikhism tended to die. You are not born a Sikh, but must be baptized therein at adult age, and the tendency of the young men was to forsake the strait path, and lapse to be, if they so wished, among the inferior Hindus. But the British officers knew that the merits of Sikhism in forming military character was very great. They insisted that any recruit born of Sikh parents should be baptized, or in the Sikh metaphor 'take the *pahul*.' This was done in full regimental 'thing'—to turn to Saxon metaphor—and with the regimental Sikh chaplain officiating, the young men entered Sikhism with ceremony. The Sikh centre, the Golden Temples and its authorities were much rejoiced, for they felt almost powerless to stem the rot that had set in. The help thus received from the Army saved the situation. Service in the British-Indian Army was very much sought after, and the certainty that the son of Sikh parents would not be taken in the 'Sikh' regiments unless he too were a Singh soon had the desired effect on a race that still had the martial tradition. Sheered up by this help, Sikhism resisted the rot, and when politics and community feeling began to head for the ballot box, Sikhism became fully re-established. But to those who watch the shaping of ends by a divinity above, the story is not without its humour.

The Hidden Paths

In this great continent with tentacles that strike far out, back into the mists of time, with all the deities, gods and godlets that the ingenuity of man and priest, and the incantations of witches can call forth, it is but to be expected that there would be many a strange secret and hidden cult. Hinduism and its all embracing genius will allow them all under its contemptuous shade. The people must be amused, and while those who are twice-born may seek the infinite by many strange and devout ways, those who are not, may weld into their cults any evil obscene or illicit practices they like. The Bhakti cult, which is the 'salvation' teaching, only wants some living drive to be all that the highest thoughts of the devout and earnest Christian could wish for. Hidden ways of mysticism flourish too in piety, under the aegis of the Brahmin and within the precincts of Islam, but at the bottom of the scale are cults more suitable to the poultry yard than the temple, in which the organs of birth, the *linga* and the *yoni*, stand as emblems and gods, and naked female beauty occupies the altar.[1]

[1] In the following descriptions apart from animism, the development of Hinduism is shown as if it was the earliest faith in India. Never-the-less, the astounding discoveries at Mohenjaro and Harahpa, on the Indus on a civilization 2500 years B.C. may throw light on some very ancient faith, to which some of the Dravidian survivals may be traced.

CHAPTER II

THE HINDU RELIGION AND PHILOSOPHY

THE DAWN OF HINDUISM—THE TRIPLE EXPANSION—THE DOCTRINE OF RE-INCARNATION AND KARMA—THE THEORIES AND PHILOSOPHIES—THE DEVELOPMENT OF THE HINDU CANON—THE HINDU CANON ITSELF—THE TEXTS AND LANGUAGE OF THE SACRED WRITINGS—VISHNU AND SIVA—THE EVOLVED SYSTEM.

THE DAWN OF HINDUISM

WE cannot even faintly grasp the spirit and enduringness of Hinduism and its more developed side Brahminism, unless we can take ourselves far back into the mists of time, and watch a great faith evolve, and a simple people develop from

"A fire mist and a planet
A crystal and a cell,
A jelly-fish and a saurian
And the caves where cave men dwell."

From simplicity shall we come to completeness, from completeness to tolerance and fancy, and the strangeness and evil of the hidden and secret cults that grew beneath the Hindu umbrella. And all the while that we watch the branch of the Aryan race that moved from the steppes to the Indus, we shall see subtle minds probing, inquiring, devising, puzzling out into a code, ideas of life and death, of god and devil. We shall see countless theologies expounded through innumerable ages, and through it all,

Brahman, the Almighty, the Essences, and the Atman developing from the crudest and earliest conception.

> "Then a sense of love and duty
> and a face turned from the clod
> Some call it Evolution
> and others call it God."

Any brief or lucid definition of Hinduism in the known language of theologians is quite impossible to make, and it can best be followed by tracing the Aryan story, and then shall we come now and again to one of those 'many mansions' of which Jesus spoke.

From the steppes to the Oxus, from the Oxus to the Indus, from the Indus to Mother Ganges, from the Ganges to the forests and regions of the devils and demons of Central India, the same instinct that sent the prows of the Western Aryans ploughing the Western seas, brings the Eastern Aryans to similar domination of the far South of India. Let us see in our mind's eye a simple pastoral white folk with their flocks and their herds coming perhaps two thousand years before Christ, up the valley of Oxus, filling up in what we call Afghan Turkestan, and the Macedonian termed Bactria. Let us imagine their waves lapping round the valleys and hills, and poking their crests into every tract that seemed worth while, surging back from the Hindu Kush, setting up in Balkh that great buttress of the centuries which held back the horde of the Folk of the Almond-eye, which science calls 'the Mongol fold.' Let us watch them slowly passing from pastoral to the agricultural state, and thence by long steps to power and dominion, growing browner in the process, as perhaps fifteen hundred years B.C. they descended from the higher plateau to the Indus, to destroy or absorb a civilization, hardly yet staged in history.

Their faith so far as they had it, was but the desire inborn of man held to be the strongest of all proofs that a divinity exists, to worship the higher powers that obviously are present, for they saw that sun, moon and stars obeyed some rules, and that there was a demon in the East Wind that men might well propitiate.

They recognized too that in the temple of the father, lay that strange spark of human life that never dies, and which is itself eternity. From this they built up that faith of the family and ancestor worship which the foolish West is losing, eventually regarding the father as the family high priest, the same idea that lies in our dying family prayers, and is the subject of a picture of this year's Academy.

The forces of nature therefore they worshipped, as the only conception they were then able to attain to, of the Power behind the Universe.

The Triple Expansion

Gradually the simple conception of the gods became more complicated, and special attributes, favourite and associate animals, were connected in men's minds with each. Gradually too a special clan or tribe succeeded in becoming the recognized priesthood, and assumed the name Brahmin, which was later identified with Brahma the Creator—God. This change covered many hundreds of years, and many changes came over the peoples as they penetrated to the south, during which the joyous life they had known in the uplands became one full of fear, fear of spirits, of demons and of ghosts that were imbibed from the folk they mingled with, ideas of the gloom of forests and the dread diseases of climates less salubrious than that of Bactria, and the hill uplands.

As a measure of salvation from the earlier experience of the direct result of miscegenation with the black and aboriginal races of India, the leaders introduced, it is believed, the great law which eventually became 'Caste'. Among the many millions the white race would be lost. By making marriage within the race essential, lay salvation for the white race, whilst outside it would be the outcaste and low-class races, from whom sprang the sixty million untouchables and the caste rules of modern days.

With these changes the gods come and go from fashion, the great *personae* of the Hindu deities as we know them now appear, and the priesthood as the centuries roll on, becomes divided into classes charged with different functions, those who sacrifice, those who sing praises and so forth, a much revered order of ascetic the *Vanaprasthra* 'forest dwellers' arise and teach in the forests, somewhere about 1000 B.C. The clearer minds raised questions continually, and devised rules of life and theories to meet the phenomena of the world and of men's hearts. The different writings begin to appear, recording what has hitherto come down by word of mouth from the priests. The idea of one deity supreme above all men and all powers develops, or at any rate a divine essence diffused throughout the world under the name of Prajapati, and this takes place about the time of Isaiah. Just as in the early days of Christianity, the elders and teachers soon found that a theology and a theory must be developed to explain the new Christian religion and the world, to thinking men, so in somewhat different ways do the Hindu teachers, sages and scholars, continue to devise and correct their earlier conceptions. As in the New Testament, and as in the Qoran, the writings come later than the teachers. As those who were orally taught pass away, so does the cry come for a record, a record of what the teaching was.

The ancient hymns of the priest that were divinely given to the seers become at last written and we have the Vedas, the first books or writings of the Hindu canon.

There are certain points that are accepted by the white race as being divinely appointed. 'Caste' as a condition of life, and the sanctity of the divinely appointed priestly race the Brahmins, while Siva and Vishnu, emerge as two great gods, which place the others into the shade. The Brahmin thinkers place them as but representatives of the Creator, as a *persona* of the Deity. But the people, especially now that by the sixth century B.C. the white race has spread so far and acquired domination over the earlier races, affected by the contact therewith, were more than ever ready to worship many gods. Among the low-caste races, especially in the villages, the gods were, and are, countless, but all recognized by thinkers as but one manifestation of the well-known gods. In the teaching of the inner reconcilization, all gods were recognized and very properly recognized, as the best that the ignorant villager could do to show his reverence and worship to the Almighty. The tend of modern thought also leans that way, viz., to accept that all those who who worship a deity are but trying to find the living God.

The educated Aryan minds long recognized this truth, and therefore swept up into a pantheon the gods, which they came to regard as but manifestations in accordance with local wont.

But such a policy also justified the tendency to any form of worship that fancy might dictate, for the god after his custom merely have appeared and intimated his wishes to certain of his followers. There are numerous parallels to such a conception in other cults and religions. It would not be extravagant to say that the village gods were not far removed from the Christian conception of patron saints, to whom humble folk attribute interventions and even injunctions. It would not be impossible to describe the Hindu pantheon as merely patron saints, and the great gods of the Temple cults only, as God, and that too as a particular *persona* of the supreme deity.

By the sixth century before Christ, the Hindu religion as thus built up was beginning to take its set form, and was getting near to the great set-back of the Protest of Gautama. How the faith was growing will perhaps be seen best by the outline of the Hindu Canon.

It will already be noticed that no mention has yet been made of any moral law. Even the most mystical teachings of the supreme deity do not attribute righteousness thereto. There is no decalogue, though countless codes of custom and of ritual. God is the embodiment of joy, of peace, of rest, but is not connected with righteousness, and there seems to be no declaration that the 'Lord thy God is a just as well as merciful God,' and has laws of conduct for men to observe, as the Semitic teaching understands the words.

The Doctrine of Re-Incarnation and Karma

With the subtle Aryan minds at work on theological speculation, it was but natural, as has been said, that a definite theory of the universe and its problems of life and death, and all that must hang thereon should be formulated. From the brains of the priesthood as of the philosopher, there evolved the theory of rebirth and transmigration, claimed naturally as revelation . . . a claim held no doubt with reason, on the theory that all great thoughts come from God . . . but claiming to be a divine revelation communicated to a seer.

With transmigration must go to complete the theory, *karma*, men's actions and reactions. Taken together it can only be said that to human minds these two theories do produce the most satisfying explanation, that the world has yet heard of, the phenomenon of life, and the inequality of measure that seems to be meted out to individuals here on earth. With the theory goes also, or has added itself thereto, the theory of the *Atman*, the world-soul, which a portion has been leased to each living thing that hath life. To everything that is born of a woman or of a feminine of a species there is vouchsafed a portion of the *Atman*. As a life sows so shall it reap. As its *karma*, its actions . . . by no means always the result of its own volition . . . so its future. The soul of man to-day may be the *Atman* of an animal or plant in another existence. Some souls mount by reason of their good *karma* to higher and higher stages, until at last they are re-absorbed. Others fall lower, and may leave the human race, the age life of a soul may be up and down, like the ball atop the water jet, now up, now down, and in any life works out the penalty of its *karma* in the last. From this arises the theory or rather the hope that it may be possible to escape from this dreary round of lives, from the retributory existences. by a short cut, by avoiding *karma*, and thus to attain the eventual absorption in the deity or the eternal world soul. *Karma* is crime, lust, passion, war and evil. Withdraw from the world and you can have no *karma*. A monk's or a hermit's life should let the fatal *karma* lie quiescent.

It is a strange compelling theory, this eternal migration of souls in an 'inner circle', going round and round, getting out at this station or that, being bundled back in the train as you want to get out, the journey going on to the ages, unless you can find the secret way to the lift that will take you to the cool air above.

As soon as we study the story of Buddhism we see the

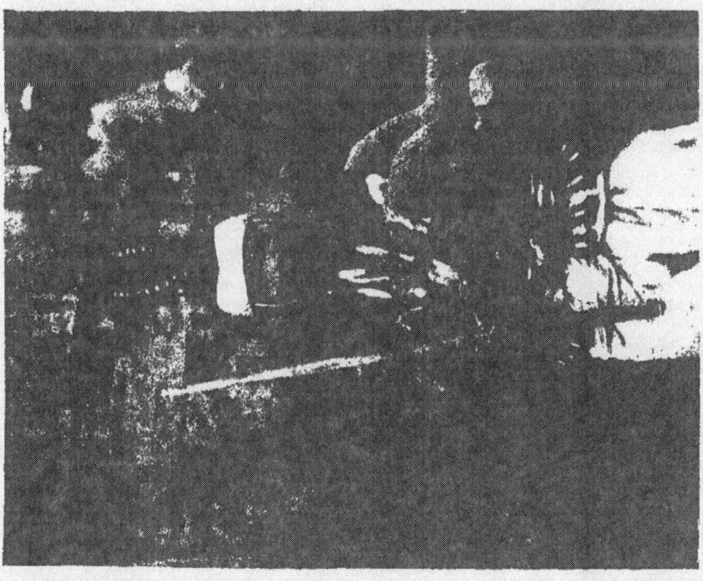

same idea controlling that faith, and *Nirvana* or *Nibbana* the state of 'no more pain' being set as the goal.

The Theories and Philosophies

Transmigration and *karma* were not the only developments in the eighth to the sixth centuries B.C. Taxila, the city at the opening of the beautiful Hazara valley, not far from the modern Rawalpindi, was the chief centre of learning, that Taxila whose ruins are only this day being dug out. It was a period of sacrifices, and the exaltation of the priest who alone could make them effectively. It was now agreed by all the deeper minds that all gods are manifestations of the absolute, but the absolute being farther away, the worship of the manifest continued. With transmigration and *karma* came also the theory of the ages of the world, the *Mahayuga* with the four *yuga*, the golden, the silver, the bronze and the iron, which come round and round too in eternity. In Brahminic theory Brahman is the *Atman* of the universe, and soon as explained was recognized as identical with the individual Atman, the soul of man.

Child marriage and the use of idolic representations of the gods are adopted. All boys of the Brahmin, Kshatrya, and Vaisya classes, the three pure divisions of the white race, attend at Brahminical schools. Methods of release from *karmas* are studied, men practise austerities to acquire supernatural powers and gifts, or else renounced the world, becoming *sannyasi* (renouncers) and *bikshus* (beggars) or *paryrajakas* (wanderers).

Six recognized systems of philosophy that are considered orthodox have been evolved and accepted prior to the Buddhist period, and from them and the teachings of Buddha and Mahavira most of the later structures emanate.

The systems that are most known at any rate to Western folk are the *Sankya* and *Yoga* systems. No earlier treatise of the first exists, but Patanjali in the second century wrote a manual known as the *Yoga Sutras.* They must all be referred to again when we come to the reconstruction and revival and what may perhaps be called the smothering of Buddhism. The teachers of the revival also belonged to that period. The systems for the most part deal with *karma*, release from the world and sin, and explanations of the phenomena of this world and what is behind the veil.

In this period in which coinage is started and the cities grow, for much the same reasons as they have grown elsewhere, the conquest of the gloomy south continues, with the absorption of its deities and dreads. About 500 B.C. Darius of Persia, also of Aryan blood, turns the north that we now call Afghanistan and the Punjab, into a Persia satrapy. The desire for release from *karma* is now growing in India, and *tapas*, austerity, is being more popularly practised to this end, rather than for the earlier purpose of acquiring power over the forces of nature. *Tapas* means monasteries and hermit cells, where men may meditate in peace. But by now two great kingdoms have arisen which war one with another. Complicated too are growing the theories and teachings of life, the systems of the philosophers and the commentators thereon. Then there comes, several centuries before Christ, suddenly as a flash to the minds of those in trouble, the 'great discovery', the real sense of a supreme God with whom men may be in communion. Brahman, or Bhagaran is joy, all powerful, and incomprehensible, but attainable. A later phrase sums up the new teaching. *Sachidannand Brahman.* 'Brahman is truth and knowledge'. This teaching emanates in glory from the Upanishads. As this teaching and its *Bhakti* emanation are those on which the fervent upholders of Brahmin thought seek to justify themselves and their scriptures in the face of Christian claims, it is better studied under the heading of modern Hinduism.

But while this great conception was dawning swiftly on the minds of the thinkers, what of the Aryan world at large, and the millions they had absorbed and were absorbing?

The answer is something as follows. To them the earlier conceptions of worship and the gods gradually developed into the expansion of two of the earlier lesser deities, into two great *personae* of the Godhead, Vishnu and Siva, almost antagonistical in the eyes of their followers, representations nevertheless that a simple man could take joy in. But before glancing at the development of Siva and Vishnu as the worship of the millions, it will be well to see the Hindu Canon as such evolving.

The Development of the Hindu Canon

We may best skim lightly over the ages which saw the evolution of a theology the most complicated and abtruse that the world has seen, by following a brief description of the religious and epic Hindu writings of antiquity. First in order come the Vedas, the ancient hymns composed by the early priests, and for many centuries handed by word of mouth and memory only. Veda means 'knowledge.'

The Veda consists of four books, and the oldest is the *Rigveda* (*Ric*=verse), and for the sake of comparison may be termed the book of psalms. From this the other Vedas gradually have been sorted out and compiled into various groups of hymns suitable for special ceremonies and occasions, much as would be the case in a modern hymn book. The three divided Vedas are, the *Samavedas* for the second order of priests the 'praise singers', the *Yajurvedas*, consisting of Vedas containing the sacrificial verses and rules for those working the services known as the 'forest' rituals. Later the *Yajurvedas* were separated into two, 'Black' and 'White,' the former containing the sacrificial verses only, the latter the whole text. These make up the three Vedas. The *Rigveda*, whence the others derive, is deemed a 'revealed scripture' being communicated by the particular *rishi* or 'seer' who originally received them from divine source. It will be seen that the mere allegation that they were divinely inspired or revealed, carries with it the idea gradually forming in the minds of the priestly theologians, viz. that behind all the conceptions of the Gods there must be a 'God Almighty' behind them all, from whom at least they derived power.

In studying all the ancient faiths it is necessary to realize that 'God' or 'God Almighty' and 'the gods' are very different things. In ancient Babylonia when the forces of nature became the tyrants or the aiders of the people, the old impression of God Almighty seems to have been clearly maintained among the cultured higher priesthood. It has been held that the great priestly college at Ur of the Chaldees, an institution of immense antiquity, at which Jepthro, the Chaldean priest who was Moses's father-in-law must have been educated, knew well the conception of the Almighty of the Patriarchs. It is most probable that Abraham himself was a student there, and learnt the same . . . the knowledge too choice for the uncultured folk, but never forgotten among the initiated.

It is even thought that Moses himself, in the years he spent with the Bedouin on the desert with his father-in-law, must have visited Ur, and learned as he was, in all the priestly law of Egypt, have sat at the feet of the priests of Ur. From there he may well have learnt the old name of God Almighty, which they called '*Eah Hueh*,' and from that produced the new ineffable name, the *Shem Hamephorash* that was the old name, JAH WEH, the WORD OF POWER, that men call the Tetragrammaton.

Further, to touch in brief on so immense a subject, the gods of all the creeds, Egyptian and Roman, Greek and Hindu, are but the same, the forces of nature whom the the people dreaded and propitiated, quite apart from the great I AM behind all the universe of whom all faiths had some dim ken. It has even been said that Nimrod the 'mighty hunter before the Lord' was *Diuspiter*, 'The Father of the Gods,' and a founder of a mighty empire, of which the story is lost. Further to his sons he gave dominion, and they have become under various names 'the gods' of all the faiths of the countries over which they ruled.

We see the same in the strange faith of the 150,000 'Devil Worshippers,' the Yezidis of the Jebel Sinjar in Iraq, who only worship *Malik Taous*, 'Prince Peacock' the Evil One, because the Almighty has handed the world to him for the current millenium, and who while *Malik Taous* reigns, will not help mankind.

So while ancient Chaldea dealt with the gods whom they knew rather than the Almighty far away, on the other hand the Aryan priests began to realize and teach that behind all was a Supreme Power, Brahm or Brahman, of whom the lesser gods were emanations and derivatives.

The *Rigvedas* appear to have taken form from the *rishis* perhaps 1300 years before Christ, about the time that Moses led Israel from Egypt, and to have been completed and the other Vedas compiled about the year 1000 B.C. when David was King in Israel.

Next in age comes the sacred writings the *Brahmanas*, which are comments and explanations on the Vedas by the various priestly schools studying and developing them. These would have appeared about the middle of the ninth century B.C., when the Iliad was being written and Elijah lived in Israel. A hundred years later in the parallel of Isaiah was composed or collected a fourth Veda, the *Atharva Veda*, embodying or giving credence to the more popular superstitions, and enumerating charms and spells to bring weal or woe. The *Brahmanas* are a dreary literature, but have some historical value as giving light on the Aryan development and movements.

Several centuries were yet to pass before the Hindu Canon was to be completed by a very different sort of writing, the *Upanishads*, which teach of the joy of being one with God, and of achieving salvation. This higher thought was developing through many conflicting teachers and many priestly schools between the years 700 and 500 B.C. The parallelism in other countries gives us Zoroaster in Iran, among the other Aryan Eastern folk, Jeremiah amid the Semites and Pythagoras in Javan.

In the many priestly schools throughout the land, as has been said, many codes known as *Dharmasastra* had been evolved. Most notable is the one known as the *Manava Dharmasastra*, the Law book or Code of Manu brought to its present form about A.D. 200. It is something similar to Deuteronomy, in that it contains countless rules of life, many of them of purely sanitary or economic intent, which were made thrice enforcible by religious precept. How many sanitary inspectors would rejoice if sanitary rules governing diet and conduct, had the driving force of religious inhibition held by a people who feared to break those rules!

Such writings as these, together with the later *Puranas*

or the chronicles of the old things aforesaid, explaining and extolling the ancient gods and their systems, are not part of the 'Canon' but are writings 'about it' and as such are widely read and revered.

Famous among the ancient writings are the two great historical epics, the *Mahabharata* and the *Ramayana*. The former is a poem that attains the immense length of 100,000 verses, some eight times the length of the poems of Homer. It probably reached its present stage about A.D. 400. The sacred and epic hymns and books seem to have been actually committed into writing about the second and first centuries B.C. During the first few centuries of the Christian Era the real and early *Mahabharata*, the epic history of wars and conquests, has been increased to four or five times the original length by the addition of instructional and other matter, and is now a mass of Brahminical injunctions. Its records are still immensely popular, and have really come in their plethora of legend and story from the heart of the people, who love the stories of god and hero which make the foundation, while the *Ramayana* which is 'the Adventures of Rama' is equally beloved. Krishna in the *Mahabharata* and Rama in the *Ramayana* begin as human heroes and eventually are accepted as gods, and both more and more important as thought and speculation on their personalities increase. Krishna the sportive romp becomes the god of joy and happiness, while Rama becomes, and is recognized with Krishna, as an incarnation of Vishnu. Both the books in spite of the accretions of the ages have many invaluable and unexplored historical secrets for those who may make critical research and study.[1]

[1] Writing in script did not apparently come into use till the second or third century B.C. As explained elsewhere the probably more accurate 'word of mouth' preserved the Vedas etc. for a long period.

The development of heroes into recognition by humans as gods, and as incarnations of a *persona* of deity, an incarnation they may not themselves have been aware of, is a feature which repeats itself through the ages of the development of Aryan theology, and in this latter connection might be compared with the theory of the writer of 'Ecce Homo'.

In considering this matter of the Brahminical and Hindu Canon the strange phenomenon of the great gap in continuity in Hinduism should be realized, unparalleled in religious history, owing to the rise of the teachings of Mahavira the Jinna, and Gautama the Buddha, already alluded to. The complete eclipse of Brahminism and Hinduism for several centuries and its eventual return strengthened by these experiences, will be told later. The gap lasted centuries, from roughly 500 B.C. to A.D. 500.

The Hindu Canon Itself

The writings which compose the *Sruti*, or canon, as distinct from the *Smriti*, or tradition, are as follows—

The *Vedas*, viz., the Rig, the Saman, the Yajur (Black and White), and the Atharvan.

The *Brahmanas* (the teachings and commentaries of the Priestly Schools on the Vedas (for the Priests).

The *Aryanyakas* (for the Forest Hermits).

The *Upanishads* (for the laity who seek salvation and happiness).

Thus they are rather like the Old Testament, divided into the Law, the Prophets and the Hagiographa, which include a good deal of history.

Close to the Canon, but not of it, are the *Sutras*, brief concise codes and sermons for the use of the priests and students, summing up for easy committal to memory, and for complete repetition, the principles contained in the rambling books of the Canon. The *Bhagavad-gita* Hymn of Adoration, greatly revered, was written in the earlier centuries A.D.

The Texts and Language of the Sacred Writings

A bowing acquaintance with the languages of India is helpful to those who would follow the religious systems. The Aryan language, that of the white peoples who from somewhere near the Caucasus or the Sea of Aral, set forth on the three eccentric world paths, as all the world knows, has formed the basis of the languages of Europe, of India and of Persia. That of the Aryans who entered India naturally developed with the growth and advancement of the people. When the Vedas were first committed to writing, the language in which they were written was immediately made static. It had become, as in the case of other such writings in other languages, a classic, its grammar being recorded by Panini of Taxila before the year 300 B.C. The spoken languages went on developing with the passage of time, but this remained, and as it was the educated language of the period it became known as the '*Sanskrit*', the 'polished language' and reached its highest stage of development about 500 B.C.

The Aryan language went on developing or deteriorating in various parts of India, and was known as the '*Prakrit*'.

But other religious writings, such as those of the Buddhist Canon and many teachers, were written at various later dates in the vernacular. As soon as a book was written that language in which it was written became a recognized, recorded, stereotyped language. From these Aryan languages, derived from that tongue of which the Sanskrit was the Indian variety, come the recognized tongues of Indians. These are Bengali, the language of over fifty millions Marathi, that of nineteen millions, Assamese, Oorya, Punjabi and the like. One of the Northern Prakrits only preserved in Burma, Siam and Ceylon, in which the famous Buddhist Canon, the *Tripitaka* or Triple Basket was written, is known as the *Pali*. *Pali* however only means 'the text,' and it is not certain which of the Prakrits *Pali* really is.

The dates of the scripts in which the records come to us is a matter of many lesser controversies, and there is room for many theories. The climate of India is against the preservation of manuscripts and thirteenth century documents are rare. That astounding preservation of documents, over five thousand years old, in baked clay, which is the feature of the past in the dry Mesopotamian climate, had no counterpart in India, unless the excavations in the Indus valley are going to open up entirely new light on the matter. In India writing had developed sufficiently for Panini to record his grammar, which was written not later than the fourth century. But the 'Rock Edicts' of the Emperor Asoka, in a script derived apparently from some Semite source, are the earliest records in India. In the whole of Vedic literature there is no evidence of a known alphabet. Even till well on in Buddhist times record was oral and handed down by word of mouth, and it has been said that this is a better guarantee of accuracy than the repeated copying of manuscripts, with their inaccuracies and glosses. The recorded text of one of the ancient writings at the time of first writing down, is likely to be more accurate than a written text purporting to be of the same early date as the oral traditions themselves, but preserved by means of copyists. The Asoka Edicts are of course an entirely different

A STONE CAR OF TRIUMPH (Hindu). (S. INDIA)

THE GUARDIANS OF THE SHRINE AT THE CAVES OF ELLORA

matter, and here again we may reflect on the advantages which the students of ancient Babylonia have in their original baked clay scripts. . . some nearly twice as old as Asoka's carving.

Vishnu and Siva

While the Brahmin thinkers were evolving their doctrine of Brahman, the Lord of all, the great mass of the people were following their many manifestations, their village and family gods, and all and any form and conception that might seem to them, to remind them best of the great power of the world. Far and wide were the Brahminic and other schools, and countless associations of monks, renouncers, wanderers and the like, under vows, and free from vows. During the centuries some deities had fallen into disrepute, and others grown popular. In fact it is not stretching the matter too far to say that the conception and name of the deity changed as the peoples aged and the races blended. Out of it all came two main conceptions, which must be viewed in the light of the Brahmin contention that all roads lead to Brahman.

The great god Rudra, long worshipped as the Lord of fear and hard things, gradually receives the euphuistic title of Siva, 'the auspicious', and becomes the essence of austerity and devotion to duty, and every idea that can be tacked on to such conception. The gods who deal with the humanities of life gradually merge into the great and kindly Vishnu. Gradually the masses of the people tend towards one group of thought or the other. Deities, analogous in their guardianships, become forms and incarnations of Vishnu or Siva. The people are either Sivites or Vishnuvites and temples, priests, schools, orders, monasteries and fraternities are all different in each worship. The religions are entirely separate and at times fiercely sectarian and antagonistic. Only can they both be classed as Hindu under the definition that Hinduism is what Hindus do, and in the mind of the Brahmin theologians that all Gods are but *personæ* of the great Deity, whom it pleases the people to worship.

Shiva or Siva is known and worshipped as Mahadeo, the 'Great God', Hindus are Sivite or Vishnuvite almost as folk in England are Liberal or Conservatives in outlook. Within both folds are many noble activities. Curious however is another development of thought. Each of the two great gods and all the lesser representations and emanations of them have their *sakti* or female side, which really represents the same ideas and attributes from, to use a modern shibboleth, 'a woman's point of view'. But as so many of the Indian peoples are sensuous and erotic by nature, so does the worship of the Saktis take many strange and erotic forms, and hidden cults, in which worship and eroticism rampant are encouraged to mingle. 'Left-handed' and Tantric Saktism are however side cults requiring when developed to excess, a very persuasive argument to justify the claim that its doings are but allegory.

The popular temples of the 'Great God' each contain the sacred emblem, THE *Linga*, in polished black basalt in weathered limestone of the male organ of generation erect and triumphant. In allegory what more striking emblem to represent the creator and eternity! To those who are childless and pray for the blessing of issue, what more potent representation of power to anoint and pray to it. Yet in the lesser vehicle of sensuous human nature what unseemly depths may be reached! To this day in every temple of Mahadeo, the lord of life and death, stands this emblem, ever present in red-washed mud under every village shrine and holy well.

I am the God of the sensuous fire
that moulds all nature in forms divine
the symbols of death and of man's desire,
I am death trod under a fair girl's feet.

And that the twain shall be one, with this worship of life and fecundity, comes also the *Yoni*, the emblem of the female organ, and the inner sign of one surrounded by nine, which must be dealt with more fully under the cults that spring from such broad conceptions.

The Evolved System

When these years of evolution and the absorption of strange cults, and ideas, briefly outlined herein, had passed, and the sacred book had been completed and the classical language built up, there stood at the beginning of the sixth century B.C. the dual system which is known as Brahminism in its higher thoughts, and cults, and Hinduism in its more popular ones. And it brings us to the question once again what is a Hindu? Hinduism is not the Hindu's term for themselves, either in ancient and modern times. In fact it is still as difficult as it was a chapter back to describe Hinduism, and the best description perhaps is that Hinduism is 'what a Hindu does'. It is conformity to the practices of those who are Hindus. To a Hindu his religion is *dharma*, which, as MacDonell says, includes established order, usage, institutions, custom, perception, right, duty, moral merit, good works and rights.

When Brahminism and Hinduism thus stand forth fully fledged, they together represent the faith which may also be described as the racial religion of all the white race in India and those who have become joined to it in some sort of religious and political conjunction. It presents theories of great beauty for the philosopher and mystic, supplemented for the "*oi polloi*", those who do the daily work of the world, by a pleasant rollicking religion, under the kindly auspices of Vishnu, or the austerer and more audacious shield of Siva. These cults are equipped with side-shows galore, which yet are within the fold, for all who are outside the normal, with also great lifting up of hands by wives and priests for those too busy to attend to such matters themselves.

The tenets of the essential Brahminism and Hinduism at this period of elaboration, before the great downfall, have been summed up as much as follows, viz. a theory of God and the world, presenting

(i) One impersonal God who alone is real, and a pantheon of manifestations thereof to suit all tastes.

(ii) A conception of the world an unreal phenomenon, with *karma* and transmigration as the basic theory of life, and release the desired goal.

Giving effect to the above is the organization such as it is, and was, controlled and based on—

> 'The inspired writings of the Vedas, the priestly race divinely ordained, the holy rules of caste.'

It is still to be noticed that though the idea of Brahman is secure in the thinkers' minds as the lord of all with whom union is attainable, yet is Brahman not connected with holiness and righteousness, and for that reason has it been remarked that the teachings of the Brahmin priests and philosophers differ in the first essential with the teaching of the prophets or seers of the Hebrews concerning the God of Israel. The absence of any central body to rule the Brahmin or Hindu faith and all the organization that springs therefrom, will be commented on when the revival is dealt with, the revival that was to take place after the many centuries during which Brahminism and Hinduism sojourned in the wilderness of oblivion and neglect which was now to begin.

CHAPTER III

THE RISE AND FALL OF BUDDHISM

THE MANY TEACHERS OF INDIA—THE TEACHING OF MAHAVIRA THE JINNA—THE LIGHT OF GAUTAMA THE BUDDHA—THE COMING OF ALEXANDER OF MACEDON—ASOKA'S EMPIRE AND THE SPREAD OF BUDDHISM—THE BUDDHIST CANON—THE BUDDHISM OF THE LATER DAYS—THE COMING OF THE TARTARS—THE GREATER AND THE LESSER VEHICLES—BUDDHISM LEAVES INDIA.

THE MANY TEACHERS OF INDIA

IN the welter of teachers, philosophies and systems which have been referred to as stirring Aryan thought in the sixth century B.C. and those following, some were destined to become famous for all time, others were to fade away. The Brahminical teaching of the *Upanishads* and the Hindu system of philosophy have been outlined. While men's minds in one quarter were set on getting into spiritual touch with a living deity, and were probing the doctrine of the world soul and man's heritage therein, ceremonial Brahminism and corrupt and sensuous Hinduism were developing apace, so that the everyday religious life became more and more set with complications. The many teachers aforesaid formulated varying theories of the world and its causes, of God and the soul, while codes and commentaries thereon grew more and more abstruse.

Power and might and dominion had supervened on the subjugation of the Dravidian races of the South, and great Aryan states, of which there were now several went to war one with another. Then began the change for which the doctrines of Brahman and the Atman and the commentaries thereon had prepared the way. About the same period came two teachers of release, both of whose schools live to this day. One is the life rule of perhaps a million and a half Aryan merchants of India, the other was destined to change the outlook of life of the East and more than the East, to spread through India and make that land its own for centuries, and then to grip to this day countless millions in the further East.

Mahavira the *Jinna* and Gautama the *Buddha* were contemporaries. The followers of any leader or teacher were apt to confer some title of affectionate respect, and do so to this day, as witness the title of 'Mahatma' conferred on the Guzerati moneylender and pleader of Lincoln's Inn, *Baba* Gandhi. Mahavira the founder of the Jains was termed *Jinna* ('conqueror'); Gautama was known as *Buddha* ('the enlightened') and others were known as *Tirthakara* ('fordmaker', 'pathshower').

Somewhere about the year 580 B.C. there was born at Kapilavastu, a hundred miles north of Benares in what is now Nepal, one Gautama, the son of Suddhodana, chief of the small Rajput tribe, the Sakyas . . . a young Rajput princelet who led the life of hunting and occasional war that such a position would indicate. The cruelty of the chase and the horror of avoidable war was suddenly born in on his mind, and he proceeded to renounce his former life, and preach what was at first a world philosophy and atheism, but as the centuries rolled on became a world religion. Like all other great teachings it had a rule of life and thought for the thinker, and a comfortable conception of life and duty for the workers and those who must make the great world move and live. The stories of the personal teachings of Gautama, as recorded through the ages, are very numerous and attractive. Gautama being himself a twice-born Hindu had no doubt the Vedantic teachings and the conceptions of the *Upanishads* before him. But he saw in the daily work around him how little 'ice' these teachings cut in everyday life. How the people were immersed in complicated rituals which puzzled them, and lived in dread of curses and evil spirits from whom their religion did not release them. He must have seen too that the world was tired of it, and longed for a better 'way'.

To show them the 'way' was the aim of this great being. Before we glance at the teachings let us digest the chronology, and realize that like Christianity it did not blaze at once through the East. It was not carried as was Islam at the sword's point; it quietly smouldered, as the elect followed the fire creeping steadily among the dry leaves and dead undergrowth of a choked faith.

The Teaching of Mahavira the Jinna

In both cases of the *Jinna* and the *Buddha* the teaching was for the people, and used the vernacular, the *Prakrits* already described, while the haughtier Brahmins kept to the statelier *Sanskrit*.

Mahavira taught that everything that lived had souls and his followers, called Jains, who survive in India to this day to the number of a million and a half, are extremely careful to injure no living thing. The doctrine of Transmigration and *Karma* is accepted by them as by the followers of Gautama, and release is obtained by asceticism. Large fraternities of Jain monks were formed. But both Jainism and Buddhism began as a philosophy rather than a religion, and imagined or conceded no living God. Jainism proved too inconvenient a rule for those who had to face the everyday rough and tumble of life, and never prospered and swelled as did Buddhism, possibly because it never seriously challenges Brahminism.

Nevertheless it remains in India proper as Buddhism does not, and is chiefly among those wealthy business men who can observe with meticulous care the injunction to take no life. Wealthy therefore have been their religious endowments through the ages, and wonderful their temples. Of their position in the nineteenth century more anon.

The Teachings of Gautama the Buddha

No religion or life philosophy can be taught unless it has an acceptable explanation of life. Gautama accepted the doctrine of transmigration and *karma* as the basis. From this, and on this, the 'Way' could be built. "One thing only do I teach, suffering and escape from suffering. As the ocean has but one taste, so my Way has but one savour, that of salvation." We thus see that Buddhism is the philosophy of enlightment, '*Bodhi*'. Gautama, or Siddartha, princelet, who is also known as Sakyamuni 'The Sage of the Sakya tribe' was the '*Buddha*', the 'awakener', the 'enlightener'. And he came to this earnest Aryan world already very much concerned with the spiritual side of life, and only seeing the greatest of them 'through a glass darkly' and very perplexed as how to find it.

At the time of Gautama's teaching there was an old Indian prayer familiar to many which ran

"From the unreal to the Real
From Darkness to Light
From Death to the undying."

When Gautama first experienced his awakening or world-call, he sought for light by attaching himself to famous teachers, and while finding often enough his problem fairly stated, he found from them no solution. Then he went forth on the Quest by himself, turning his back on asceticism and the selfish life of he who would sit alone, saving his own soul perhaps, but caring naught for the great world in travail. At last after long search and pondering and self discipline, he himself reached a holy calm. He had reached that state of Nibbana or Nirvana (in transliteration of Aryan terms 'r's and 'v's and 'b's interchange very easily), that state of peace which in other words the Bhakti seeker had found, when his soul or Atman mingled with the world-Atman. In achieving this state it seemed to him that transmigration and the craving for the world were over, over for him. Then he proceeded to teach. He seems to have codified his own experiences and from them laid down four great axioms as the fundamentals of Buddhism.

(1). All things are sorrowful, (for the world is out of order).
(2). There is a cause for this disease.
(3). The cause is Thirst or Craving (*Tanha*).
(4). The cure for this disturbing thirst is the Noble Eightfold Path.

The 'Noble Eightfold Path' was epitomized thus:

Right Understanding.
Rightmindedness.
Right Speech.
Right Action.
Right Living.
Right Effort.
Right Attentiveness.
Right Concentration.

The paths were grouped in three groups, 'Enlightenment, Morality, Concentration'. Each were subjects on which an infinity of subsidiary teaching could be given, both by the Buddha and through the ages. This Eightfold path is in effect a ladder of the Mystic, complicated enough, but far simpler than anything that Hinduism has evolved, and uttered as Hinduism did not, a note that is moral in its way of life, and which definitely connects religion and life together.

As with the Gospels and as with the Qoran, the teachers wrote nothing down. It came by memory and word of mouth, and it was not till one hundred and eighty years after the death of Gautama that any attempt was made to write down and codify the teachings.

It is evident therefore that there was plenty of room for divergences, innovations and glosses. Apart from the simplicity of the doctrine, the known and affectionately remembered character of the Buddha, simple, kindly and unselfish, was a clearly delineated picture. His teaching was of a nature dear to all Hindu thinkers, and it is not to be wondered at that it spread, and eventually, but not for many generations, swept India. The following extract from one of the *Suttas* [1] gives an idea of his personality as it appeared to those who passed it on, as well as of his actual teaching.

The conversation is related as taking place in a monastery in a certain park. The 'Blessed One', Buddha, addresses the monks.

> "I will teach you oh monks the burden . . . the bearer of the burden, the taking up of the burden, the laying down of the burden.

[1] *Sutta* is the Prakrit form of *Suttra*, the name for the short Brahmin codes, which are short hymns, codes and stories of the Buddhists.

"And what oh monks is the burden?

"Reply should be made that it is the five attachments. And what are the five attachments? They are: the form-attachment group, the sensation-attachment group, the perception-attachment group, the predisposition-attachment group, and the conscious-attachment group. These oh monks are called the burden.

"And who O monks is the bearer of the burden?

"Reply should be made that it is the individual; the venerable so-and-so of such and such a family. He O monks is called the bearer of the burden.

"And what O monks is the taking up of the burden.

"It is desire leading to rebirth joining itself to pleasure and passion, and finding delight in every existence . . . desire for sensual pleasure, desire for permanent existence, desire for transitory existence. . . This O monks is the taking up, called the taking up of the burden.

"And what O monks is the laying down of the burden?

"It is the complete relinquishment, forsaking and non-adoption of desire. This O monks is called the laying down of the burden."[1]

The Coming of Alexander of Macedon

At this stage it will be convenient in following the slow but certain spread of Buddhism to glance at the Indian chronology of the six centuries before the Christian Era. The birth of Gautama is put at 557 B.C. and his death in his eighty-first year at 477. While his teachings were slowly absorbing India, there came a great and romantic happening, the invasion of India by land by Alexander of Macedon. Having conquered the Persians he entered

[1] From p. 159, Warren's *Buddhism in Translations*.

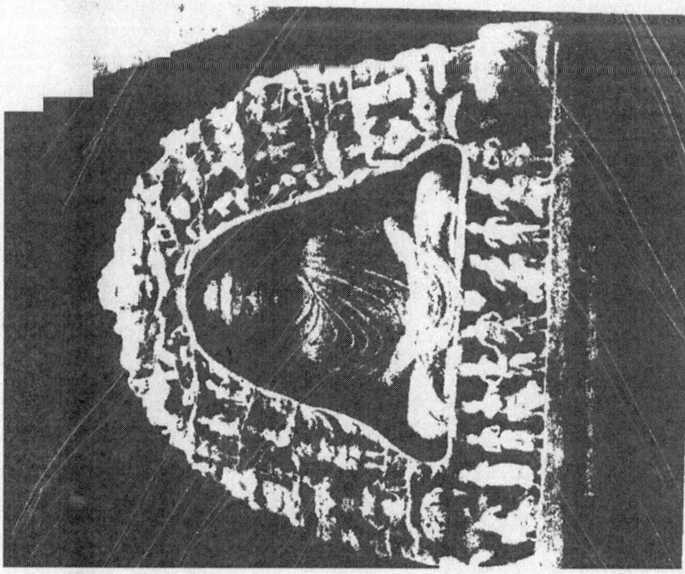

the Indian Satrapy of Darius, and at Kabul in 327 B.C. summoned the Princes of the Punjab to acknowledge him, the successor to the Persian throne, as their over-lord. As they failed to comply he advanced on India, not as is often supposed by the difficult Khaiber, but crossed the Kabul river near Jellalabad, and eventually entered India somewhere near the Malakand. Before crossing the Indus he turned aside to storm that Rock of Aornos, so long a mystery and bone of contention to archæologists, which Sir Aurel Stein has recently discovered in territory only accessible of late years.

Alexander then crossed to Taxila the capital of Taxiles, later a great scene of learning and Buddhist piety, which the Indian Archæological Department has recently been excavating. Taxiles, it may be remarked had accepted already Alexander's summons to allegiance. We need not pursue his progress further, except to remark that Buddhism was not yet the commanding religion of the land. Alexander left in India what in modern Army parlance would be called his 'C3' men, those unfit to march home, and returned to Babylon where he died. There then arose in India a young Indian soldier of fortune who swept away the Greek *régime* in the Punjab, wiping out or absorbing the garrison, and the Indian troops with Greek officers. This young soldier had been hand in glove with Alexander in proposing further adventures, and is known to Greek history as Sandro-cottus, and more correctly as Chandra Gupta, who, after the Macedonian's departure, gained his object, the rulership of Magadha, of which Patna, then Pataliputra, was the capital. But though the Greek races were submerged in India the Greek kingdom of Bactria, under Seleucus, one of the Macedonian leaders, remained, and Alexander's venture had brought the two civilizations together.

Seleucus also invaded India, penetrating to the Ganges where he found himself in such difficulties that he agreed to surrender all the North of India as far as Kabul, and gave his daughter in marriage to Chandra Gupta, who received a Greek ambassador Megasthenes, at his court. From Megasthenes we learn something of the history of India, and of Hinduism, in his account of his five years' sojourn at Chandra Guptas' capital, learnt in Greek too, long before the translation of Sanskrit documents gave us corroboration and details. His accounts however contain much that is elfish, especially when he writes of wonders he had not seen but had swallowed. Buddhism he never mentions and Chandra Gupta was certainly not a Buddhist. Chandra Gupta reigned four-and-twenty years as king of Magadha and overlord of northern chiefs and lesser kings, and he founded what is known as the Mauryan dynasty, destined however as the Lancashire saying has it, to return to clogs after three generations. Nevertheless the third generation, his grandson Asoka was to found the first and one of the few really Indian Empires, and to be undoubtedly the greatest ruler India ever had till the coming of one of the greater British viceroys.

His Empire now marched with the Greek kings in Bactria, and the mingling of the civilizations was to have lasting effect.

Asoka's Empire and the Spread of Buddhism

In the year 272 B.C., Asoka ascended the throne of the Mauryas, and spread that dominion over a large part of the south of India, and raised his Empire to a pitch of civilization and prosperity. So notable a personality was not likely to be unacquainted with the kindly philosophy which was now beginning to spread. In the ninth year of his reign Asoka became a Buddhist. Later he even became a monk, and he has been called 'the Constantine of Buddhism'. A religion adopted by the ruler of an Empire must get a great fillip therefrom, and Buddhism, at this period half way between the birth of Buddha and the birth of Christ, now rapidly spread over all India to Ceylon, to Burma and Siam. Brahminism was driven from the field and became of little account.

In this period stone architecture came into fashion, and we have the carved Buddhist temples and monuments, many of them beautiful and elaborate which exist to this day. Rock inscriptions make their appearance and all over India have been found edicts engraved on stone by order of Asoka, setting forth the main rules of life and character, instilled by the Buddhist faith. But Buddhism had already gone a long way from the simpler teachings of its founder. Being like Islam and Christianity, a missionary religion, rather than one primarily reserved like Judaism and Hinduism for a chosen people, it did of necessity acquire something from the people to whom it appealed.

The teaching was, as all such teachings have seemed to be through the ages, incomplete at the outset. They must be supplemented by a theory of life to which they belong, or they must fit into some existing theory. Gautama, as has been said, accepted transmigration and rebirth as the theory of life and *karma* as the reason of evil, even while his thinkers naturally re-arranged their conceptions of both doctrines, just as modern Christian thought is modifying the thoughts and ideas of such questions as hell-fire.

The subtle Aryan mind found plenty to elaborate in all that Gautama had left behind: plenty of blank spaces in the sequence of logic that must be filled up, and we can watch among other things the gradual changing of what was an agnostic philosophy and 'way' to a religion, wherein the belief in presence of a Brahman, a *Yahweh*, which an instinct in human nature demands to be conceded, gradually takes shape again. The same pervading presence that had taken control of Brahmin thought begins to dominate Buddhism.

The power or desire to build in stone, produced in India marvellous work and ornamentation, while the art of the inscriptions gave a new way of publicity. But we find statues of Gautama becoming statues of a God to worship, rather than a memorial to venerate, and shrines become temples. India is still full of rock hewn temples, shrines and stupas of the Buddhist period, simple at first, growing more ornate, in which scenes in the life of the Buddha are portrayed, and many of the famous and captivating incidents of his simple life and career are recorded, as well as representations of followers venerating the teacher.

The first attempt to codify the teachings were instituted by Asoka, one hundred and eighty years, as has been said, after the death of the Buddha, and thus was the Buddhist Canon formed.

The Buddhist Canon

Rock Edicts themselves in some sort, may be looked on as one of the bases of the Canons, prescribing the tenets and the way of life and right doing. The Bhabra Edict in Rajputana, contains the well-known formula of faith in the Buddha, in his teaching, and in the order. But the principle among the old writings that form the Canon, is that which comes from Ceylon, which is still a home and a centre of Buddhism. It is written in the vernacular of the period, now known as *Pali*, because as explained in Chapter II it was the stereotyping by writing of one of the Aryan languages as it was then, *Pali* as already explained but meaning the 'Text'. The Canon is known as the Three Baskets or *Tripitaka*.

The First, the *Vinaya Pitaka*, is the Discipline Basket, and deals with the rules of Monastic Life, divided into three.

The Second, the *Sutta Pitaka*, or Sermon Basket, contains the teachings of the Buddha, divided into five.

The Third, is the *Abhidhamma Pitaka*, the Exposition Basket, and is the expansion of the explanations of the Buddhist teaching and doctrine, divided into seven.

In addition to the Tripitaka there are innumerable writings written during a considerable period, of great sanctity, some of which are almost within the Canon. Such a book would be the *Milindapanha*, which records the conversations of one of the Greek Kings of Bactria State, by name Menander with a Buddhist elder, from whom he is inquiring. Of this, the following extract shows the charm.

Said the King "Bhante Nagasena, what is the reason that men are not all alike, but some long-lived, and some short-lived, some healthy and some handsome, and some ugly, some powerful and some weak, some rich and some poor, some of high degree, some wise and some foolish?"

Said the Elder, "Your majesty, why are not trees all alike, but some salt, some bitter, some pungent, some astringent, some sweet?"

"I suppose Bhante because of a difference in the seed."

"In exactly the same way, your majesty, it is through a difference in their karma that men are not alike, but some long-lived, and some short-lived, some healthy and some sickly, some handsome and some ugly, some powerful and some weak, some rich and some poor, some of high degree, some wise and some foolish. Moreover, your majesty, the Blessed One has said as follows: 'All beings, O youth, have karma as their portion; they are heirs of their karma, they are sprung from their karma, their karma is their kinsmen, their karma is their refuge, karma allots beings to meanness or greatness'."

"You are an able man Bhante Nagasena."

The Buddhism of the Later Days

With Asoka searching for the original Canon, with the truth and the truth only being proclaimed, with all the force of the whole Empire behind it, it is not to be wondered that the faith spread. The country from the Hindu Kush to Ceylon, saw the art of Hindustan at work on making its great stone records of the golden age now past, but almost within human memory. Monasteries full of monks seeking release, studying the way, and teaching the laity arose in every direction. The retreat from contact with the world indeed, resembled very much the same sort of movement as took place later in Christian lands, and obviously meets a trait that is widely spread in human hearts. To this day wherever Buddhism exists, there are monks, and in Tibet and especially in Lhassa, which has been called the Vatican of Mongolian Buddhism, monks and nuns form a very large part of the population.

Just as the desire for pilgrimage to the holy places neither existed nor was in demand in Christendom till several centuries after the life of Christ, so only now were pilgrimages to the holy sites of Buddha's life the fashion. The Boh Tree under which Gautama gained enlightment, the Deer Park in which he resided and taught, and any other places famous in his life story were eagerly sought.

But as has been said the busy Aryan mind wanted more information then the teacher had thought necessary to give them. More depth and distance was necessary in the philosophy. And eventually was evolved the teaching that Buddha was only the incarnation of the Great Spirit vouchsafed to this age. There had been other Buddhas in the past and there would be more in the future. It has been said that Buddhism, at one time an agnostic philosophy attempting to do the work of a religion, at this time developed the beginning of a worship. Images were made of the twenty-four mythical and previous Buddhas as well as of Gautama, the historical Buddha, and even of Maitreya the future Buddha, at the stupas, in pagodas and chityas. While originally put up as stimulants to meditation, they soon became objects of worship to the general public, and offerings of fruit and flowers, tapers, incense, and all the paraphernalia of the worship of a divinity after the lush methods of the East, were introduced. With these came more systems and more philosophies and Buddhism began to resemble the Hinduism against which it had been the revolt.

The history of India went on from incident to incident, more exciting and upsetting than had yet been seen, the Maurya dynasty failed and wilted, and many states took its place.

The Coming of the Tartars

During the decline of the Maurya dynasty, the Greeks from Bactria set up many small states west of the Indus. In Ghandara, which is now represented by the Swat Valley north of Peshawar, a considerable Græco-Buddhist civilization arose which contains to this day remarkable Buddhist remains in which Greek art is much *en evidence*.

Great events however were moving in Central Asia. The Parthians from Persia were pressing on the Greeks and a fierce group of tribes, the Sakas, driven westward by pressure of the Tartar tribes of the Yuechi, entered northern India, breaking up the Indian states of the Punjab, and penetrating to Kathiawar. From A.D. 21 to 71 it appears that a Parthian king, Gondophares, ruled on the Indus, and there is indeed a tale that he received a visit from St. Thomas on his way to or from the South of India. Gondophares must have gone down before the Tartar Yuechi who, under Kadphises and the Kushan tribe, conquered what is now Bokhara and Afghanistan. His son Kadphises II, conquered India as far south as Benares, and his grandson Kanishka succeeded in A.D. 125. Under the Tartar infusion of new blood and drive among the Aryans, a powerful and enlightened kingdom arose in India with capital at Peshawar. Kashgar, Yarkand and Khotan were added by Kanishka, who himself became a zealous Buddhist and helped spread Buddhism which now gained more and more ground on the great basis laid by Asoka. But Buddhism had by now strayed still further on the path away from the teachings of Gautama. Kanishka summoned the last Buddhist Sangha or Council held in India, to settle the many disputes in progress. But we can see that change in progress even here. The

ANCIENT BUDDHIST TOPE AT THE FAMOUS SHRINE AT SANCHI

language used was the stately Sanskrit again and not the homely Prakrit. The Brahmin ascendancy was returning, there was now a definite schism between north and south, and Buddhism was preparing for the flit that was to take it among the folk of the almond eye to whom it seems to be more especially suited, for it was in Kanishka's reign that missionaries were first sent to China.

The Greater and the Lesser Vehicle

The schism that has just been referred to, is the division of the Buddhism of that day into what is known as the *Mahayana* or High Path or Greater Vehicle and the *Hinayana*, the Low Path, or Lesser Vehicle, the schools of the North and South, the terms *Mahayana* and *Hinayana* being somewhat terms of reproach. The Buddhism of the High Path teaches salvation by means of the Buddha through the ages, who has become almost a 'salvation' God. Guatama taught that it lay within man himself. Here we see adumbrated in some sense the difference between a 'catholic' and a 'protestant' conception of the Christian Verity. The last state of the Buddhist to which a man may attain is now twofold, that of the Arahat, the monk in contemplation who in kindliness and gentleness has attained *Nibbana*, while the *Bodhi-Satva* is a new conception, he who prefers not to go to Buddhahood till all the world can go with him, but has become a saint helping those still travelling, and was in fact worshipped as a God. The calm and peaceful figures seen so much in Ghandaric remains are not as a rule presentments of the Buddha, but of a Bhodhisatva, looking down in pity on the world. Paradises were now offered to which men might attain and dwell in company with Bodhisatvas and Buddhas before proceeding to the far off Nibbana.

The paradise thus revealed is termed Amitabha, where previous Buddhas dwell. In the *Amita yur dhyanor Sutta*, the sorrowed Queen is shown the paradise that awaits the devout, where souls meet again.

Even in Asoka's time previous Buddhas were being recognised, now the great theory of twentyfour, already referred to, is established. The faith was busy absorbing atmosphere from the mentality of its converts, and from contact perhaps with outside. Mithras for instance touched the Indian boundary, and while Hinduism might consider such a diety as but a form of Brahman, Buddhism could conceive an early Buddha, and so we have practically come to a salvation religion, and one in which the Buddha was 'compassionate' as well as enlightened.

Unfortunately Buddhism was also imbibing the sensual and erotic imagery of Hinduism, and when we come to consider 'enlightenment' in modern times we shall see four different schools of varying moral worth, and be inclined to confess that the Mahayana when kept pure and unsullied, is more human, more compelling and more satisfying to the ordinary human mind, than even the simple ways of Gautama's teaching.

Buddhism Leaves India

With the passing of Kanishka the last drive temporal passed from Buddhism. The dynasties that now gained power, notably, the great one of the Guptas were Hindu and the Brahmins were able to exercise some pressure. Buddhism also had become so full of ceremonies and pomp, processions of previous Buddhas and the like, that there was not much to choose between it and popular Hinduism. But as taken to China by Kanishka's and subsequent missionaries, it had there a great future, appealing in the simplicity with which it was spread to many men of learning. In fact as it died in India it spread to the whole of the Far East, the *Hinayana* going to Burma and Siam, the *Mahayana*, but in its simplest and best forms, to China and Japan. The monasteries and Pagodas in these lands to this day stand in places of great beauty, veritable abodes of peace, and though not the universal faith, Buddhism is held by many of the best and wisest as well as the simplest in the land. Modern Buddhism as a religion and a cult with its schools of thought and teaching, is a very live factor in these countries and will be dealt with later on, when we consider these religions as they stand to-day, deeming Burma and Ceylon as India for our purpose.

It has been said and probably with some truth, that Buddhism is the religion that suits the psychology of the Tartar and almond-eyed races best, especially those who are mountain dwellers, and therefore given to meditation and perhaps melancholy. Islam and the Judaism of the flat-nosed Tartar Jews of Russia appears to be made for Semites, and to be out of place in a Tartar psychology.

The fulfilment of the Buddhist dispensation in India and its waning, comes to us somewhat vividly in the diaries and itineraries of certain Chinese Pilgrims, who came to India over the Karakorum and through Kashmir and down the Indus to visit the sites and scenes of the Blessed Ones life.

The first whose record we have is Fa Hien, who left on his return in A.D. 414. Fa Hien had travelled and studied in India for fifteen years, and speaks of the glory and splendour of the great arts that flourished, of the carvings and paintings in the pagodas and shrines and the rock-hewn temples, employed by the Abbots of monasteries and the wealthy laymen. The power and learning of the monks of Ceylon impressed him greatly, and in many monasteries both the High and the Low Path teaching flourished side by side. But he describes, nevertheless, a lush and decadent Buddhism, full of magic, of ceremonies and the ways of Hinduism.

We now turn over the pages of two centuries to the itineraries of Houen Chang, who travelled between A.D. 629 and 649, and from them we get pictures of the decay. He finds noisy disputes in progress everywhere, between the Buddhist and Hindu teachers. Many of the monasteries are half empty and the whole picture is a sad one for an ardent Buddhist pilgrim searching for the way, and trying to follow the 'Noble Eightfold Path'. Human nature is back again where it started on the quest. There were notable exceptions here and there, as at the University of Nalanda where Houen Chang studied. The accuracy of these records have been cross-checked in several ways, and have lead to archæological finds in our own time. Most notable is that of the gold casket with some bones of the Blessed One, discovered as the itineraries said they would be, in the stupa of Kanishka outside Peshawar,—a grey mud mound that the ages had let severely alone, with none so poor as do it reverence—though it had been the most famous site in Northern India.

CHAPTER IV

THE RETURN OF HINDUISM

THE GUPTA DYNASTY AND THE TARTAR—THE COMING OF THE HUNS—THE RECONSTRUCTION OF HINDUISM—THE TEACHERS OF THE RECONSTRUCTION—RAMANUJA AND NILAKANTHA—HINDUISM IN THE MOSLEM PERIOD—THE RESULT OF THE RECONSTRUCTION—THE TEMPLES—THE JAINS DURING THE EPOCH—THE UNTOUCHABLES.

THE GUPTA DYNASTY AND THE TARTAR

IT is not possible to separate religion from temporal history, when dynasties are falling to invaders, and new races arrive that tear every structure to pieces, and to follow that final collapse of Buddhism and the re-birth of popular Hinduism, we must listen to the clanging of arms and see the web of politics.

Kanishka the great Kushan Emperor died in A.D. 150 and was succeeded by his son Huvishka, who seems to have had equal respect for the gods of many religions. But the days of the Tartar dynasty were numbered, and by the middle of the third century the Kingdom of Magadha was once more rising to power and dominion, under another Chandra Gupta, the petty prince of what was once the famous dynasty. His conquests were so extensive over other kings and princes that he assumed the title of "King of Kings" in 320. He was himself a Hindu and paid great respect to Brahmins though not unfriendly to the Buddhists.

His descendants were even greater monarchs, and in 375 his grandson Chandra Gupta II came to the throne, still further extended the Gupta dominions, and the old peace of the Buddhist era was gone. Nevertheless Chandra Gupta II, who had assumed the title *Vikramaditya* ("Sun of Victory"), gave the country forty prosperous years, and did not interfere with the Buddhists enjoying that autumn of their prosperity which Fa Hian saw. The Gupta Empire indeed now fell little short of Asoka's in extent and in prestige. Kumara Gupta succeeded to Chandra Gupta in 413, but during his reign fresh combinations and groups of Tartar barbarians commenced the inroads of the Kushan type again. Shanda Gupta ascended his father's throne to find himself involved in a long and costly struggle, which he conducted gallantly enough, gaining in 470 a victory over them, which gave peace for several years. When he died in 480 his exhausted empire fell apart. The Guptas were all zealous Hindus and during the generations of their power Hinduism, and Brahmin influence, grew to be the popular and fashionable religion.

The Coming of the Huns

In the beginning of the sixth century the Tartar scourge came again. Defeated in Europe at the decisive battle on the Marne, they recoiled into Central Asia, whence they broke South into India under Toraman, sweeping through the country with terrible force and outrage, destroying many a Buddhist monastery and stupa. In 510 Toraman was succeeded by his son Mihiragula, whose reputation for cruelty and excesses exceeded that of any of his forbears. Happily a combination of Hindu chiefs and princes gained a victory that gave rest for many years, though Mihiragula himself succeeded in ousting the ruler of Kashmir, and starting a fierce persecution of Buddhists, styling himself a follower of Siva. Happily he died shortly, and power seems to have fallen into the hands of a Hindu king Vasodharma, who in finally expelling the Huns has become a somewhat mythical national hero, to whom also the title of *Vikramaditya* was given. Series of Hindu kings and quarrels supervened, and eventually at the beginning of the seventh century Hindu Harsha founds what is practically an Empire of the North. This brings us to the time, already referred to, of the Chinese pilgrim Houen Chang. It was the effect of the Hun invasion a hundred years earlier, from which Buddhism never really rallied that produced the decadent state of affairs which the pilgrim recorded. Nevertheless, as Houen Chang relates, he found many wealthy kingdoms established notably in Malwa and Gujerat. From the driving out of the Huns, to the coming of Islam from the north in the middle of the eleventh century India had rest from invaders though hardly from herself. Since the days of the Guptas, the Hindu revival had been daily gaining power and weight, and Hinduism was now to a considerable extent, the national religion once again, and a dynasty founded by Harsha of Kanauj now gained the principal place. Before we glance at the reconstruction, there is one more historic incident connected with Buddhism worthy of note. Harsha died about the year 648, after a prosperous reign of fifty years. A man of learning and piety, he had surrounded his court with the learned and gifted. But endowing Hinduism largely, he left an empty state coffer behind him, a sure pointer to discord. His Minister, Arjuna, a keen supporter of Brahminism and an active enemy to Buddhists, usurped the throne. Soon after his accession, a companion of Houen Chang,

Wang Houen Tse by name, arrived in India. Arjuna seized all he could find of the mission and put them to death. Wang Houen Tse escaped to Nepal. The rulers of Nepal and Tibet, both Buddhists, hastened to avenge the unforgiveable injury. A small force of mountaineers invaded India and defeated in Tirhoot a large Hindu force under Arjuna, who was himself captured and led away to China, never to be heard of again. Wang Houen Tse later led another mission, whose reception was all that could be desired. With this well accredited incident the curtain drops on Indian affairs, and remains down for close on two hundred years, during which apparently the Hindu states of India fought together and evolved a working situation, unco-ordinated by any great empire builder or world-stormer from within or without.

The Reconstruction of Hinduism

The problem before the Brahmin hierarchy of maintaining their hold, and of the reconstruction of Brahminical and popular Hinduism must have been a remarkable one. It is of course necessary to realize the very long periods of years over which brief accounts skip with apparent simplicity. From the birth of Buddha to the death of Harsha is a period of twelve hundred years, a period as long as that from the end of the heptarchy in England to the present day. When Buddhism was at its zenith in India, which was not till perhaps five hundred years after its founder's birth, if not more, Brahminism must have been at a low ebb. Numerous Brahmins and almost all Hindus must have embraced the new faith. Buddhism nominally at least, abjured caste. It is however to be presumed that the caste instinct remained as, in more modern times, it remains illogically among Moslems and

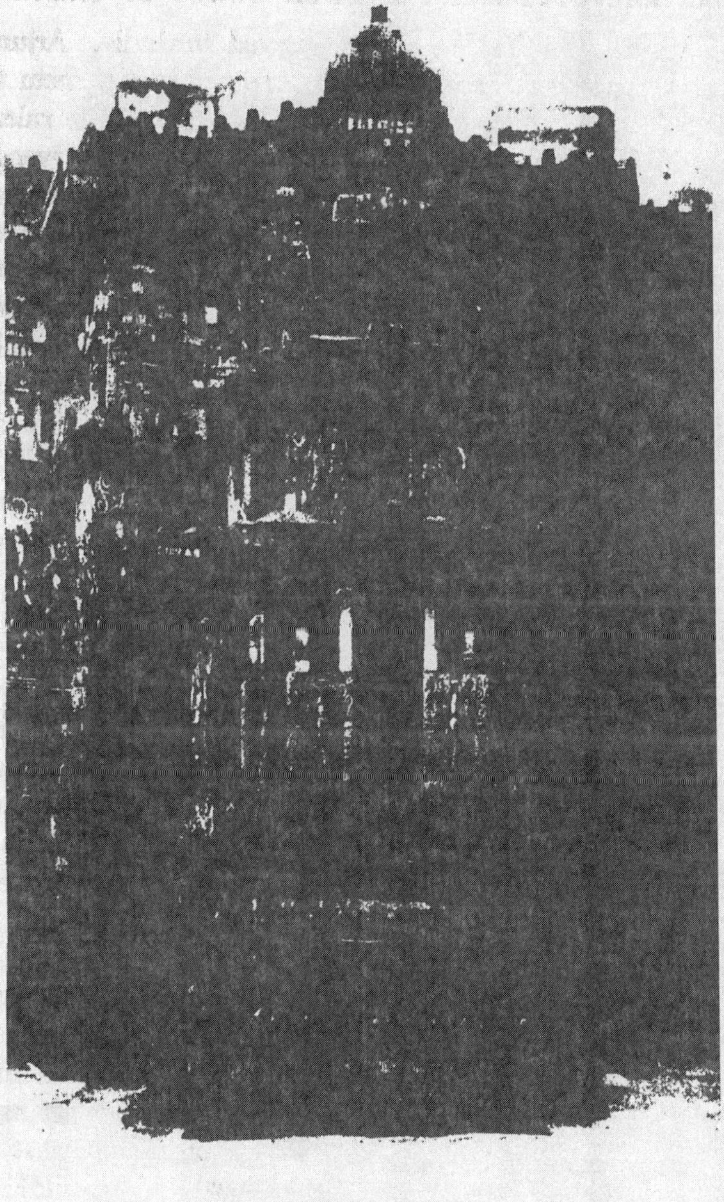

ORNATE HINDU TEMPLE AT HALÈBID (MYSORE)

Sikhs, and that it was retained as a social institution, in the same sense as to this day marrying out of one's social grade is a shock to many people in Western lands. But nevertheless countless folk must have lost all caste barriers, although the power of the Brahmin to keep his identity even under persecution is remarkable, and we have an instance of this in Kashmir. There are no Hindus now indigenous to Kashmir, once a centre of Hindu learning, save the Brahmins. Here although the ordinary folk were converted to Islam many a century ago, the Brahmins or at any rate a strong nucleus of them surviving preserve all Brahminic thought, even in the days when they must have been comparatively isolated from their own world. However it came about, the old castes were regrouped, assuming once more religious form and sanction, over what had remained for centuries social tradition. The high twice-born castes re-took their historical place tempered by expediency. Many non-Aryan tribes were admitted into the caste system, all weighed, graded and placed by a mixture of priestly craft and moral worth, and political consideration, tempered by public opinion. Very many aboriginal or Dravidian people in touch with civilization now came into such of the caste system as was open for them, the lower and contemptible position below the Aryan line being theirs, but satisfying in that there were many placed far lower. As the fashion grew to be Hindu instead of Buddhist, so a Hindu status was sought after, no matter how humble so long as it was recognized, and gave admission to the temple services and the ornate public festivals of the seasons, and the like, which were now becoming the prominent feature of the new Hinduism. The Brahmins had acquired much wisdom and cunning in watching the ways of the people through the ages.

While the adoration and salvation ideas that brought release, were as much treasured in high caste circles as in the old days, the cults for the people followed, but with greater enthusiasm, the old worship of the kindly Vishnu or the more determined Siva. To the followers of each cult, Vishnu or Siva was the supreme god, the adorable deity, in other words, to the theologian, the *persona* of Brahman that seemed to the worshipper to suit his outlook on life. Among the thinkers the effort was made to introduce as doctrine the conception of the Trimurti, a Trinity of Brahma the Supreme, and the more accessible *persona* of Siva and Vishnu. Carved presentiments of dignity and beauty of the Trimurti appeared, and though this conception may be said to remain as a satisfying solution of the oneness of the supreme deity, it does not appear to have been much dwelt on, in any form of worship or philosophy. By tacit consent it remains behind all Hindu conception, since the latter, as already explained, accepts any God who may be popular, as the Deity conceived by any particular point of view. All see the Supreme Being through a glass darkly, or according to the lights that nature has given.

Working on these lines the great framework regrew, and gradually filled in its detail, which varied north, south, east and west. From the defeat of the Huns to the coming of Islam, as has been said, India's outer history is comparatively uneventful, and all the mass of foreign settlers left in the wake of Menanders, Kanishkas, Toramans and Mihiragulas, had to be re-absorbed into the warp and weft of the land. Since Hinduism was the political power, and Hinduism the only religion now left for all who would be in the swim, they too were taken *en bloc* into the caste machine, though how long it may have taken no one can tell us. The terrible system of untouchability also rose again (p. 89). Buddhism still remained in pockets, but its beautiful temples were mostly pulled down, used for other purposes, or left in ruins, though happily, at Buddh Gaya and Sanchi, the remains still show for us the beauty and glory of human thought in that age.

The Teachers of the Reconstruction

During this period of reconstruction from A.D. 600 to 1200, apart from the welter of schools and interpretations which came to no lasting fame, there stand out certain great and famous teachers, and many books in Sanskrit, explaining and interpreting the ancient writings and amplifying the Vedas. During the period also developed the conception of the female side or wife of the deity, and the idea grew that the god was unapproachable, but that the *Sakti* or female side brought mankind in touch with the deity, an idea that of course underlies Mariolatry in Christian thought. It was now that the Saktas, the worshippers of Kali grew to such importance especially in Bengal, and formed the right-handed and left-handed Saktas referred to. As has been said, the cult of the left-handed Saktas is most immoral, as well as largely concealed, and more will be said of it later. Both the Sakta groups have borrowed much from aboriginal practices and influence. The services of Vishnu, Siva and Kali, the wife of Siva, now demanded rituals and these were duly developed, those for Vishnu *Pancharatra Samhitas*, for Siva the *Saiva Agamas*, while all the Sakta rituals were *Tantras*. A university even at Vikramasila on the Ganges developed this latter strange form of adoration.

The old six Hindu philosophies were revived, but only two had any popularity, viz.: the *Karma Mimansa* and the *Vedanta*.

The famous teachers were known as *acharyas*, and taught all over the land. Kumarilla was the famous exponent of the *Karma Mimansa* the 'work enquiry,' who flourished as early as 700, and then there appeared the famous Sankara whose fame is greatest from his commentaries on the Vedanta Sutra, the Sermons from the Vedas, the Bhagavadgita and the Upanishads, he taught that nothing is real save Brahman, and that the soul of man is identical with the eternal spirit. The world is *maya*, 'illusion'. Sankara also taught the doctrine of the *Trimurti* the Hindu triad and that Brahma, Vishnu and Siva are but the manifestations of a great supremacy Brahm or Brahman. Up and down the land he went, preaching his teaching, opposing the countless sects that thought otherwise, and founding many monasteries for the encouragement of learning.

But the Sankara teaching did not square with those who preached Vishnu and Siva as the living cheerful gods that made life for a man worth living, and it was several centuries before the great man that they looked for appeared. Down in southern India there had been twelve poets who preached a popular Vishnuvism, drawn from the old *Puranas*, which taught of merry Krishna the lord of the milk-maids as well as more serious things. Written in Tamil, they were beloved of the southern people, and are often called the Tamil Vedas. In the same period some exquisite Tamil hymns were written of adoration to Siva, known as the 'Divine Garland' and 'The Sacred Utterance', both in use to this day in the Sivite temples. In north India appeared the *Bhagavata Purana*, which was in praise of Krishna, now coming to be regarded as an incarnation of Vishnu, later, about 1100 came the *Gita Govinda*, also of Krishna, who incidentally has a famous cowherd mistress Radha, which is in full erotic strain, and which, like *Le Cantique des Cantiques*, can only by the greatest imagination be regarded as allegorical. Several attempts to denounce caste were made, but nearly all after a flourishing generation or so, could not resist the caste urge so inherent in the Aryan complex. At Kalyan a Mahratha statesman founded a democratic sect to worship Siva, with a turn also towards Vishnu, devoid of all flummery, and in opposition to Brahmin domination. This sect remains to-day, and are known as *Lingayats* because a model of the male organ or *linga* is always carried on the person, as a reminder of the Creator, 'Remember now thy creator in the days of thy youth'.

Ramanuja and Nilakantha

Mention has been made of the long period that was to pass before any teacher arose who would refute the cold metaphysical teaching of Sankara, and teach as in the old time before that Vishnu meant the joy of life to all and sundry. But roundabout the year 1100 comes Ramanuja, head of the poets who sang of Vishnu and high priest of all the Vishnuvites of the south. His commentary on the Vedanta is very different in spirit to that of Sankara. Vishnu is the great supremacy in accessible form. Man's spirit is a portion of God, but even in final union maintains its own individuality. The doctrine of incarnation is very definitely taught. But although Ramanuja as a twice-born man could only speak the revelation faithfully to twice-born, that is to say, high-caste men, nevertheless, he took a kindly and sympathetic line with the outcast. Some, he even admitted to temples, and he taught them the doctrine of Vishnu as he understood it, leaving it to them to gain such content as they might by imitating the worship of the caste men. What he thought it might avail them, outside an improvement in the joy of living, history does not apparently say. But the teachers before and after Ramanuja all taught *Bhakti*, viz., that through adoration of Vishnu or Siva, mankind who were in caste, might attain salvation. And the joyous teaching and hymns of Ramanuja are in force to this day.

After him we see a somewhat attractive argument. His following fell apart into two schools, in the north called *Vada-galai* in the south *Ten-galai*. The northern school held that divine grace was 'co-operative', that is to say, that man must bear his share. The southern school say that it is 'irresistible', and falls on a man, a passively involuntary resignation like the Grace of God that passeth all understanding. Both schools accept the *Bhakti* doctrine of faith, love, adoration. The clever Brahmin theologians have styled the northern teaching the 'Monkey' school, since the monkey clings to its mother, and the southern the 'Cat' school, where the mother does all the carrying.

The Sivite school has somewhat different theology. Its prominent *acharya*, Nilakantha who has formed the real Sivite doctrine, taught that Siva is identical with Brahmin, and is a personal god but that the human soul is distinct. The incarnation of Siva is not accepted, but Siva appears in many forms to his worshippers.

It is interesting to note that these teachers seem to keep their doctrines for the inner ring of the learned and devout, for they took in all the temples services of the humble and merry, worshipping the many gods, no doubt because all gods but represented the one, and because they knew that the people must be kept content and interested in performing their allotted tasks in life. And who would have it otherwise? But as one studies all these tangled and conflicting theories of life and death and the Almighty, one can but wish that some Gibbon had written for us the 'Rise and Fall and Re-Birth of Hinduism'.

Hinduism in the Moslem Period

Between the years 1100 and 1200 came the sweep of the Moslem invasions through the hills of Afghanistan, with all the drama and tragedy outlined in the next chapter. The Moslem came as fierce Crusaders, or rather 'Crescenters', urged by a wild desire to compel all men to Islam and to destroy all idols and idol worshippers. Buddhism which still lingered disappeared, and Hinduism was seriously checked in all development. Only in the south of the 'Deccan', did one Hindu kingdom, Vijayanagar, survive the swamping by the billows from the north which rising itself in the fourteenth century stood to the storm for over two hundred years. Thousands of Hindu temples were destroyed, monks and priests were slaughtered and hundreds of thousands of Hindus slain. Nevertheless, under the heel of oppression, Hinduism and Brahminism but pushed their roots deeper into the soil, even if the outer growth was stunted and many followers left them. But the Bhakti cults grew, and most of the teachers impressed on their learners that the God of their fancy, Vishnu, Siva or Brahman was to be adored, not for favours to be received, but because as God, he must of necessity, be adored by his followers.

The two religious movements fell into groups, that of Rama the popular hero of the Ramayana now recognized as an incarnation of Vishnu, that of the equally popular Krishna also now considered to an incarnation, while a new group was evolved from the astounding and admirable deistic teaching of Kabir, whose followers were and are known as Kabir-punthis. The chief teacher of the cult of Rama was Ramananda a follower of Ramanuja's church in the south who broke away and came to the north, while following Ramananda was the popular and well-known Tulsi Das who flourished about the time of Akbar at the end of our Tudor days. To this day Tulsi Das is the favourite guide and teacher for Hindus of the north, with his famous work, *The Lake of the Deeds of Rama*, in which Bhakti teaching predominates. Both the cults of Vishnu and Siva in their latest form were open to the lesser as well as the three twice-born castes, but caste itself remained as it still does.

The famous Kabir was a follower of Ramananda, but he developed a teaching that was practically a religion of his own. He wrote fierce polemics against caste, and condemned idolatry. His followers were both Hindu and Moslem, though the former were almost all low caste. Incarnation also he strictly denied, though the Kabir-punthis insisted in regarding their leader as an incarnation himself. His teaching was pure deism, and eventually it threw forth its far more sturdy child Sikhism. Yet Kabir was a leader and character of great charm and sweetness to be admired by all men and creeds.

The Result of the Reconstruction

The Hinduism as reconstructed up to the coming of the Moslem conquerors and developed under the stunted conditions that prevailed, is very much the Hinduism of modern times, except in those small circles where Westernism has entirely altered the outlook. It had then and has now, two great branches, that as held by the twice-born, and that as held by and permitted to, the folks of the low castes, and catered for, and may briefly be reviewed as follows.

At the head of all is the philosophy and beliefs of the Brahmins in Brahman and the one God Almighty under several aspects. Secondly come much as before, the two great divisions into the followers of Vishnu, and of Siva, the former usually in the form of Rama and Krishna, the high caste in both cases believing in *Bhakti*, adoration of and salvation through the deity. In each case we find the mass of the people and all the humbler castes worshipping, more and more flamboyantly as you go lower, the two greater and countless lesser deities, whom scholars explain as but conventions of Vishnu or Siva, or else demons and spirits to be placated. In the south amid the lower castes of Dravidian race, the worship gets more and more savage and fiercely primitive, and is nearly always tinged with greater or less eroticism.

Among the educated, many schools and variations of belief prevailed, ahead of the popular beliefs. As through the ages, the Brahmins were revered as super-saintly beings, whether priestly or otherwise, and on all occasions of rejoicing the feeding of a large number of Brahmins was regarded as a sacred duty.

Yet throughout all the growth of thought and custom neither Brahminism nor Hinduism had never produced any central authority, no creed and no law of good and evil. Hinduism embraced a thousand different Hinduisms, only held together by the conforming to established custom as regards the sanctity of the family, the sacredness of the Brahmin, intense reverence for the cow, and observance of the old rules and customs regarding food and marriage.

Yet for all this, among people of ordinary status the system produced a working rule of life, in which the 'original' good is more pronounced than 'original' sin. All around as now, the good people of the country side, when unmolested by Mogul and Mahratha, carried out their daily avocations, in a simple life that had many admirable sides. The priest in his temple and the wife before her household shrine carry out that duty of uplifting of hands for those who are otherwise engaged. Village life and the quiet by-lanes of the city saw a happy kindly life in progress. Nevertheless Hinduism did and has done nothing to protect its adherents, especially those of aboriginal origin and humble status, from the intense dread of spirits, ghosts and demons, which in many ways made life intolerable, and gave many opportunities to the unworthy and mercenary priest.

The gravamen of the ancient charge against Hinduism, however, lies in those years, as Miss Mayo lays it still, if in less degree, to barbarous and ruthless rules of life and customs, or to customs, the mishandling of which, as in child-marriage, arouses no indignation. Also lies the charge that the priesthood have often cruelly and brutally borne such a share as is more redolent of the groves of Astaroth, or the sacrifices of children to Moshesh, than to the ceremonies of the most intellectual people in the world.

As has been said, no evil and abnormal practice so long as a Hindu conforms, is too evil to condemn. It is probable that a man might introduce and initiate a following to seances of the wildest and unimaginable bestiality, which the Hindu world would accept as the result of a god appearing and so ordering.

The inhuman and difficult customs, the side shows and the erotic cults deserve an insulated chapter to themselves.

The Temples

To Vishnu and to Siva beautiful, ornate, luscious and indecent temples, were erected by the pious, varying in taste according to the race and antecedents and internal

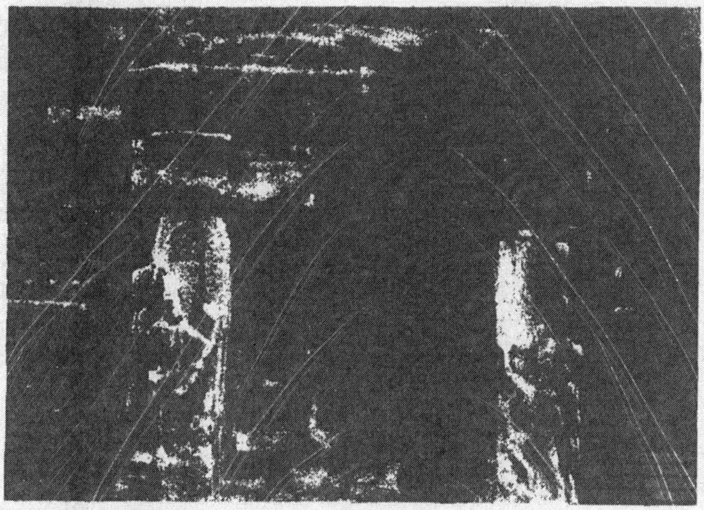

A CORNER OF ONE OF THE "DIFFICULT" TEMPLES, MADRAS

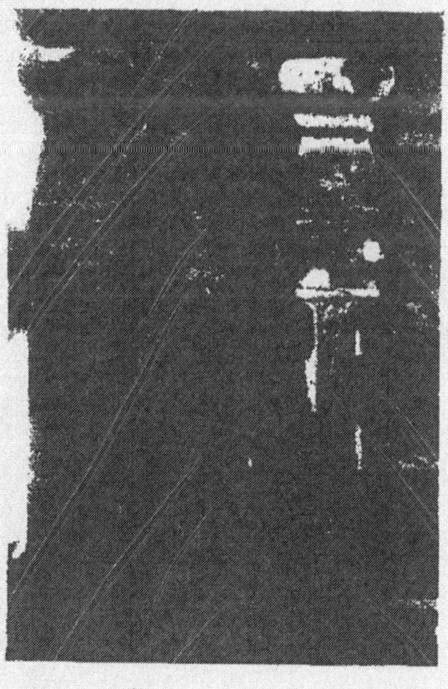

SOME OF THE LUSH ELLORA CARVINGS

psychology of the admitted races. Many orders of priests, ascetics, monks, and hermits grew and re-grew, with their large accession of lay brothers and wandering members known as *Sadhus*, *Sannyassis*, *Bikshus*, *Bairagis* and the like, whose peculiarities will be explained later.

The early temples of the Buddhists were, as has been said, the first buildings of stone. With the Hindu revival, all the old ways of sacrifice in the open, of temporary silvan shrines of the hermit forest dwellers and the like disappeared. The stone temples or those later of brick and stucco appeared thoughout the land. Those in the north were severe, austere, and often majestic, usually having the tower or spire as in the Buddhist days above the stupa or shrine. In the south where Dravidian art and mysterious cults dominated taste, came the building of ornamental temple towers covered with the most ornate carving, detailing the life of the god, stories from the Mahabharata, the Ramayana and the like. In many cases in the south, the worship of life and death and the creator took the shape of carving organs of generation, and scenes of copulation of men, of beasts, and even of humans and beasts interwoven—carvings which to Western ideas are obscenity and license unimaginable, but which as already stated modern Hindus endeavour to explain away by suggestion of allegory.

The northern Hindu temples built during the early days of the reconstruction, that is to say about A.D. 500 to 600 of stone, are much to be admired. They are to be seen in their best among the Kashmir ruins, and in some of the old temples in the Punjab, notably at the Kafir Kots on the Indus, the temples at Martand, and in the more finished work to be seen in the post-Buddhist work that is at Taxila. But in this connection it is to be remembered that the Moslem iconoclasts were singularly complete, as witness the destruction, as wanton as that of Cromwell's troopers, of the beautiful temple of the Sun at Martand in Kashmir. The country is studded in the hill regions with the rock-hewn temples, Hindu, Buddhist and Jain, of astounding merit artistically, while in seeing the great Dravidian temples of the south, the stranger can but marvel at the piety that has devoted so much wealth to the purpose. The temples in Madras, or Gopurams, are usually surrounded with a vast wall, so strong that they have often been used as forts.

So it is that in some places the temples raise stone and gilded towers to the skies, in others, in the wake of the Moslems they lay shattered and forgotten, and once again let us listen to Lyall as he speaks in the voice of Siva.

> "Let my temples fall, they are dark with age
> Let my idols break they have stood their day,
> On their deep hewn stones the primæval sage
> Has figured the spells that pass away,
> My presence may vanish from river and grove
> But I live for ever in Death and Love."

Jainism During the Epoch

It has already been explained that Jainism was an offshoot of Brahminism, like the teaching of Buddha, and was an uprising against caste. There must have been many systems and movements of the same type, and it is not clear how this particular one survived as well as Buddhism. Though it survived, it never accumulated the great driving force of Buddhism, but during the reconstruction period it increased, and remains in India the faith of perhaps one and a half million much respected people to this day. Like Buddhism it was an agnostic philosophy to begin with. It has been said that it lies midway between Buddhism and Hinduism in its philosophy, and this is not unreasonable definition. Like Brahminism and Buddhism it accepts *karma* and transmigration as the explanation of the world, and like Buddhism seeks *Nirvana* or release. It sees a soul in every living thing, including plants, even the smallest insect, being the home of a soul. It practises far greater austerity than Buddhism and is intensely careful to take no life. The irksomeness of this rule, as said earlier in this book, has proved an inhibition to the working classes from professing a daily rule so difficult to them. In common with both the two religions aforesaid *Yoga* the practice of secluded meditation in certain postures is followed. Mahavira the founder, took twelve years of ascetic seclusion to attain *Nirvana*, and therefore Jainism imposes this condition on its followers.

The Jain Canon, known as the *Siddhanta* or *Agama*, was framed at the council of Vallabhai in A.D. 454, but tradition says the council but reaffirmed what was accepted nearly seven hundred years earlier, by the council of Pataliputra held in the reign of the Maurya king Chandra Gupta. Jainism early broke into two distinct bodies, of which perhaps the special distinction is the determination to always appear naked, which distinguishes one of them the Digambara. Monasteries and nunneries flourished. The canonical Jain must possess right faith, right knowledge, observe right conduct and the five points, viz., abstention from killing, lying, stealing, sexual intercourse and all attachment to worldly things especially possessions. Laymen need only observe these points so far as the condition of their lives permit, but the injunction to kill no living thing, is however, strictly binding on all. The Canon is written in what is called *Ardha Magadha*, the language in which Mahavira taught, and besides the

Canon and many *Sutras* or sermons the lay literature is very considerable. About the end of the eleventh century lived and wrote the celebrated monk Hema-chandra, his most famous work being the *Life of the Sixty-three Great Men*.

The Jain religion like Buddhism developed a special form of art, which the wealth of its votaries enabled them to develop in their rock-hewn temples, some of their towers being specially famous as well as the paintings discovered of late years. The Temples at Mount Abu, in the Aravalli hills, are famous throughout the world, especially the astoundingly carved white marble dome in one of them.

As the years rolled on, the inherent desire for some spiritual belief also affected Jainism, and incarnations of teachers began to be believed. Twenty-three mythical patriarchs (*Tirtha-karas*=path finder) before Mahavira, came to be regarded as gods, to have temples erected to them in which their *eidolons* stood. As a quiet douce folk, they did not come into any great clash with Islam, and their temples do not seem to have suffered to the extent of the Hindu edifices.

The Untouchables

Through the ages, the grouping of the untouchables will have been noticed, those of non-Aryan race, who have been brought into the system for servile purposes, and grouped, under the drip at the very edge of the Hindu umbrella: contemptible, unsave-able, but thrice-useful. Exactly where low caste ends and untouchable begins, is perhaps hard to say. In all its mental cruelty, untouchability remains to this day.

CHAPTER V

THE COMING OF ISLAM

THE BEGINNING OF THE FAITH OF THE SUBMISSION—MAHMUD OF GHUZNI IN INDIA—THE CONQUEST OF INDIA BY THE MOSLEMS—THE MOGUL DOMINION—THE SHIAH STORY—THE ISMAILIS—THE MOSLEM CANON—MYSTICISM IN ISLAM—THE ORTHODOX SCHOOLS AND SECTS—ISLAM AND CHRISTIANITY.

THE BEGINNING OF THE FAITH OF THE SUBMISSION

WHILE Buddhism in India was going down before the recurring wave of Brahminism, and that faith was rising enriched in the soil cleansed by Buddhism, there was appearing a new star and a faith which was to further enrich Hinduism and Brahminism, while dealing it the cruellest and most ruthless blows. As it arose so it remains, antagonistic in all its thoughts and ethics and in its severe monotheism, to every conception of popular Hinduism, although Brahminism as we have seen, in its pure state can lie in sympathy with every creed under the sun.

The rise of *Al Islam* the 'Submission!' i.e., the submission to the will of God, arose as all the world knows from the teaching of the 'Prophet' Muhammad, the son of Abdullah the son of Abdul Muttalib, an Arab of the tribe of the Qoreish who had in their charge the ancient Arab temple at Mecca, which contained the Ka'aba, an old black sacred stone of antiquity; (Ka'aba meaning 'cube.') The Arabs acknowledged in some vague way the existence of the supreme deity whom they knew as Allah, who formed and ruled the world, and that was all there was to it. Each tribe had its own presiding Jinn or spirit, and in the Ka'aba were three hundred and sixty idols of jinns, spirits, lesser gods and the like. But the Arab world largely tribal and pastoral was constantly in touch with civilization, the Decapolis of Transjordania, and with all the come and go of the trading world. At this period the sixth century A.D., Christian missionaries had traversed the East, and the religion of the *Nazaras*, or Nazarenes, the word that still endures for Christians to this day, had swept over Syria and across Persia to China. The Arabs were familiar with some of their teachings, and they were also more in touch with the Jews driven from Judæa and resident in Transjordania, and who incidentally they cordially disliked. Monotheistic teaching was thus before them, the Jewish missionaries were as active as the Christians and had converted some of the Arabs, but the Christianity, that impinged on Arabia, had long been lush and none too inspiring.

Muhammad was the servant of a rich merchant's widow and traded and travelled on her behalf. Born about A.D. 571, very little is known of his life till the age of forty. He had married his mistress when he was twenty-four, was addicted to desert journeys and solitude, and had a dream or a vision, which was repeated till he became the recipient of messages from the Angel Gabriel. The interest here, is to notice how the God of the Hebrew patriarchs and of Israel, was mistily the Allah who reigned in men's minds in the Semite countries. Communicating his dreams, and what had now become his divine mission to his friends, he proceeded to teach the true knowledge of the forgotten god, who shared the Arab world with jinns and idols. Thus was emphasized the old truth, 'There is no god but Allah,' always the cry but rarely the practice of the old pagan Arabs, to which was soon to be added the necessary corollary 'and Muhammad is his prophet'. But this prophet had little honour in his own Mecca, mocked and persecuted were his followers, until a man of influence, one Omar, joined him, when his teaching began to spread. It was about 610 that his teaching began; by 622 it had become sufficiently powerful to threaten existing interests, which forced the prophet and his following to save themselves by clearing out from Mecca and going to Medina for safety and peace. From that date the second great religion of the world is dated, viz., 622, the year of the Hegira or Hijra, 'The Flight'. From that date, too, the simple desert faith and philosophy was to change. Stirred by hate and ill-treatment it became a great militant movement, and roared through Arabia.

So much the common facts of this beginning, related here but to show the skeleton of the growth as has been done for the Hinduism, that arose hundreds of years before.

The ground of Arabia and the East was ready for some such movement. The races seemed not prepared nor suited for the gentler teaching of Christ. But ready to surge they were, and a fierce enthusiasm arose which carried the belief in the only God as they conceived Him, all-wise all-powerful almighty and all-knowing, across Asia and Africa. Away all luscious false gods and idols! away all complicated lives and luxuries. *La Illah La, Il Allah ho. O Muhammad rasul il illah.* There is no God but Allah and Muhammad is his Prophet! It roared and surged across Asia like a forest fire. With it was preached the reward, a reward of earthly desires for all who fell in the great mission to spread this truth born of desert communings.

In the new temple of Allah[1] at Mecca, the *Ka'aba*, the black stone cube, too old and too knowing to be ousted, remains to this day as the luckstone of the new faith. The three hundred and sixty idols aforesaid were thrown as paving stones to the temple court, where they, too, remain still, but to be trampled on under the feet of the believers and to be spat on by all of any zeal. The sword slew its hundreds of thousands of those who would not believe. The fierce desert Arabs seized the women of the lands they conquered, and bred to themselves countless young Moslems, to be professors and soldiers of the faith of Islam, 'The Submission'. It is a strange wild story, so different from the slow, persistent and, for long, kindly spread of the Faith of the Nazarene, and it ministered to men's desire for war and glory and possession, as well as to the desire of the desert souls for a living God they could realize.

How in a very short time there arose the Arab Empire—for a while perhaps the greatest the world has seen—and how almost immediately the insistent controversy in all man-led religions arose, is now to be told.

Who was to carry on the succession as the leader? From the controversy arose the great schism which also survives to this day, and has perhaps saved Christianity for the gentler portion of the world. Three 'Successors,' or 'Caliphs', were at first chosen fairly amicably, from among those who may almost be called the 'apostles', the intimate companions of the Prophet. Dissension had existed among the followers however, as to whether succession should be by election or run in the family of Muhammad. Twenty-four years after his death, the third of the Caliphs Othman was killed by revolutionaries,

[1] Allah was the old Arab name for their priestly deity, among the idols, and hence the force of this *Kalima* or short creed.

and Ali, cousin and son-in-law of the Prophet was declared Caliph. After a stormy dominion over half the conquered territories Ali was murdered. Hassan, the elder grandson of the Prophet, the son of Fatima by Ali, was chosen to succeed, but had none of the qualities and was poisoned by his wife. Hussayn the younger was eventually supported by one faction, but perished with most of his relations at the battle of Camel, heavily outnumbered in the deserts on the Euphrates, after which the Caliphate went according to the will of the majority. But the Shi-at-Ali or party of Ali, who held that succession must be hereditary, was firmly established, and remained in bitter opposition as 'Shiahs', to the orthodox party or 'Sunni.' Ere long, as will be seen later, they developed doctrines and outlook, which still further estranged them from the orthodox. The deaths of Hassan and Hussayn, the grandchildren of the Prophet, in the struggle, has been an eternal bend sinister across the Dominion of the Faith, but still the orthodox Arab legions swept on, and penetrated far into Central Asia. In that province of early India which men call Khorassan, was found the tribe who claim descent from Afghana a grandson of Saul, a prince and a leader in Israel. They embraced the preaching, which also spread to the hardy Aryan clansmen in the hills of the Kabul Kohistan, and the mountains of Soloman. Buddhism the gentle faith went down before them, and gradually, though we know not the process, the mountains of what is now Afghanistan, the plains of Afghan Turkistan and the great flats across the Oxus, became one with Islam. Samarkand became a great centre of Islamic piety and learning, as did Meshed and Herat and many another Central Asian city. The struggle for the Caliphate or successor-ship to the head of *Al Islam*, need not be detailed here, suffice it to recall that the great Ommayad dynasty was founded in 661 when Muwaiva became Caliph of all Islam. It was during his sway that the whole land between the Oxus the Indus and the Persian Gulf and even North Africa—acknowledged the Arab supremacy. In 750 the Caliphate passed from the Ommayad of Damascus to a line known as the Abbassid of Bagdad, founded by a descendant of the Prophet's uncle, Abbas, and rose to even great fame, till it died away before the Turks.

It was, however, many generations before the conquering wave swept over the Afghan mountains and flowed through the passes to the banks of the Indus, probably because the mountaineers were absorbed but slowly. India, therefore, for a long period stood high and dry, beyond the reach of the fiery Moslem warriors and their crescent banners.

From Bussorah, which men now write Basra, indeed penetration did come, but it was very limited. It was not till 711 that an attempt was made to reach India, and an expedition following on an argument regarding the capture of an Arab vessel by Hindus, brought Arab troops under Muhammad Ibn Qasim, to the mouth of the Indus. The Hindus suffered a severe defeat at a fortified temple, probably Dwarka, and the survivors were pursued far up the Indus, Multan itself being eventually conquered and all towns of importance on the river. For forty years the Arabs ruled what is now Sindh, and then were driven forth. No further attempt to bring the Moslem power, temporal or ecclesiastical, to India took place till the end of the tenth century. Traces indeed of the Arab there are in the Indus boatmen, who resemble so greatly the hardy Arabs that ply a similar trade on the Tigris. The Baluch tribes in the mountains above Sindh are, too, seemingly of Arab descent but from some other source than the coming of Ibn Qasim.

Mahmud of Ghuzni in India

Islam be it remembered grew to be, and remained through the centuries, the faith of an Imperial conquering people. It came with the sword and it went by the sword, without temporal dominion it came not at all. Staff and wallet and the cairn by the pass, brought it not, pilgrim and ascetic came not as missionaries. By the end of the tenth century, a Turkish dynasty of power and imagination, a centre of Moslem glory, and learning had been established in the north-west mountains of India bearing nominal allegiance to the Caliph at Bagdad. The Indus valley was Hindu, and Hindu and Buddhist still held the valleys and roads that led to Kabul from the Indian plains. If the Moslems invaded over the Indus, then Northern India struck back. India proper was now once again a collection of Hindu kingdoms, but all fiercely jealous one of the other and often concerned in bitter internecine wars.

At Ghuzni reigned Sultan Mahmud, hero of many Moslems' songs and stories, the son of the Turk or Tartar Sabaktagin. The idolators on the Indus and beyond irked his enthusiastic soul. It was with him as with Falstaff at Gadshill, 'Young men must live and gorbellied knaves with fat purses are fair game'. But in his case it was Moslems for whom the fat Hindu purses should exist. So Sultan Mahmud Ghuznavi, as the Moslem poets describe him in a name that seems to sing itself, poured his Turkish and Afghan troops and his Arab descended settlers, down into the land of the five rivers and into Hindustan. The *Musheriq*, the man who shared his worship among many gods, was a foul abomination. Having conquered the Rajput armies and princes who had dissipated their own strength by their civil wars, he slew by the hundred thousand and he carried off the young of both sexes by the tens of thousands. The idols and temples of India he destroyed and rooted up with fierce hatred. *But-shikan* the Idol-breaker, is his proud title, and to this day the mounds of holy Mutra on the Ganges are strewn with the ancient carved gods and loves of Krishna, from the Hindu temples. 'The light loves carved on the temple stones' he swept away as dross before the broom. He invaded Kathiawar to destroy super-sacred temples of Somnath, whose idol treasure house he looted, and the sandalwood gates of the temple did he carry away to his mountain home of light and learning at Ghuzni. Twelve times did he pour into India to wreak his wrath on the infidel and idol-worshipper and enrich his colleges, libraries and mosques, but he stayed not to conquer. It was the wealth and lives and not the land of India that he desired. Many a man was converted by force, and forcible conversion often meant rough-and-ready adult circumcision at the hands of jesting conquerors. His prisoners and captives of course entered the fold, and Moslem historians love to dwell on the vast holocausts of infidel prisoners, no doubt to some extent exaggerated. In any case the story is always told with glee and enthusiasm, so that it may well be that there is a subconscious as well as a conscious memory that rankles, even as the North of Ireland hates the South for its pre-Cromwellite pikings.

The Conquest of India by the Moslems

While Hinduism and Brahminism are religions of the Aryan people, and the philosophy of Buddhism rose from the same source, the cult of Islam had, as has been shown, a very different origin, born indeed of the desert, with Christianity and Israel in some senses as god-parents. It was a religion which must essentially be a state religion;

Church and State are inseparable in true Islamic ethics, and Islam is based as much on temporal as on spiritual dominion. Its inherent property is and was the fierce zeal of proselytism. Its enthusiasms drove its adherents to conquest and inspired them with the *élan* thereto.

Mahmud of Ghuzni passed away, and twin sons reigned in his stead till one murdered the other, and then turning his father's policy of raid to that of conquest, established a capital at Lahore in India as well as at Ghuzni, and eventually made that former city his main centre, conquering the Punjab and penetrating to the Ganges, destroying the Hindu Rajahs of the Punjab states who attempted resistance. This great dynasty lasted till 1186 a period of two hundred and twenty-four years, spreading from the Oxus to the Sutlej and beyond. During this period a large portion of the people of Northern India had accepted this faith in the one God as taught by the Prophet. And they accepted the faith for many reasons, partly from fear of death, partly to side with a winning star that had arisen, and partly and indeed this point needs to be realized, because here was a simple faith that a man might understand, and was very different from the lush stuff that popular Hinduism implied. Like Christianity it brought hope in this world and the next to the humble and meek, and all that were desolate and oppressed. Like Christianity, it taught the slave and the outcaste that God cared as much for him and his soul as for the highest in the land. The contemptible untouchable, whom the Aryan spurned, became a child of God. When the first fierce wave of conquering Arab might had swept over the world, the age of 'the Faith or the sword point' passed, non-Moslems might live under the sway of Moslems and live their own lives, provided they paid the *jiziah*, the non-Moslem poll-tax. But it was a better life to be with the conquerors and swagger and lord it with them. Thus many Hindus of the North readily accepted Islam, both on the days of Ghuznavids and later, and among them those Rajput clans who to-day form the pick of the Punjab yeomanry, and who have born such a share in the world war against the unholy claims of the Sultan of Rum (i.e. of Turkey) to declare the cause of the Central powers a holy war.

During the latter years of its existence the dynasty of Sultan Mahmud Ghuznavi was being driven out of its mountain provinces by another mountain and Turkish dynasty, that of the over-lords of Ghor that lay in the hills south-west of Ghuzni. Muhammad Ghori eventually conquered Lahore too, and became Lord of the Indian Empire of Ghuzni. Further and further into the Peninsula he ventured, conquering the Hindu Rajah of Delhi, and carrying out an extended massacre of Hindus at Ajmere. He died in 1205, and was succeeded by his Turkish slave Kutub-ud-din Eibak whence began the dynasty of the Turkish Slave Kings of Delhi.

We need not follow the story of Islam further. Never again was a Hindu dynasty to rule at Delhi or indeed to hold sway in India. With the conquerors there poured into India, Turks or Tartars, Afghans and Persians, to gain military fiefs, to set up independent Afghan kingdoms, and to build castles and strongholds of Islam all over India. Nearly always were the dynasties Turkish, and many a Turkish noble held sway under them. The Muhammadan population of India to-day is over seventy millions and is described racially as Mogul, Pathan, Sayad or Sheikh. That is to say descendants of Tartars, Afghans or Pathans, (viz., the people who speak Pakhtu), of Arabs, and fourthly, of those who accepted conversion euphuistically-known by the holy name of Sheikh. Since Islam was the ruling faith, so state endowments to that religion grew and prospered. Great principalities were established in the south by Moslem adventurers usually Afghans, especially in Bengal and in the Deccan, where their buildings are some of the finest in the world. At Beejapore the dome of the great mosque is as big as that of St. Peter's at Rome. Everywhere between the twelfth and sixteenth centuries the Moslem dominion, backed by hordes of Afghan and Central Asian soldiers, spread its rule and its faith, aided by the more than enthusiastic converts. These Muhammadan kingdoms in the south however rarely came under the sway of the Tartar dynasties at Delhi, till the coming of the last and greatest.

The Delhi dynasties, Slave, Tuglaq, Khilji, and the like, all Turk for the most part persecuted the Hindus at intervals relentlessly, always exacting the hated *jiziah*. Nevertheless we find Rajput soldiery, especially those of Oudh and Behar, fighting under their banners far up on the Oxus frontiers, faithful like the cat, to the house rather than to the master. The dynasties of Northern India were not immune to newer invaders from the north, who preyed on them and on Hindu alike. Through the centuries the Tartar races had thrown up a succession of world-stormers, usually pagan, and in later times partly tempered by Islam, a faith whose warlike tenets did not interfere with their world-storming principles. In 1338 Timurlane erupted into India slaying vast numbers of his captives and in Delhi carrying out a massacre, of which folk still speak with awe. Yet Timur was an enthusiastic supporter of Islam in his capital of Bokhara.

The Mogul Dominion

In 1526 arose the last and greatest of the Turkish dynasties, that known to Europe as the Great Mogul, and to

India as 'Chagatai' after the Turkish province which gave them birth. Baber, a descendant of Timur, and also of Ghingis Khan, through his mother, was far more Turk than Mogul but called himself Mogul or Mongol, because this was a name of fear. Through the centuries the thought of a Mongol coming had ever blanched men's faces. As a descendant of the massacring Timur, he conceived that he had more right to the Delhi throne than the effete dynasty in possession, and down he swept with his Turks and his Mongols and any lad of spirit who would hack his way to power. How he swept over India and how his son Humayun lost it all, and his grandson regained it, is outside the margins of the book. Suffice it to say that his grandson Akbar as is well known, was the greatest ruler in India of modern times, comparable perhaps to Asoka. The *Ain* or code of Akbar, has the same famous status as the *Code Napoléon* in Europe. He it was who would have put an end to the age-old sores between Moslem and Hindu, and in that effort married *inter alia* ninety Rajput princesses. He also welcomed to his court religious leaders of many kinds, and even endeavoured to start a new creed that should embody the excellences of all. This apart from the difficulty of selection, involved him in many troubles especially with the Moslem hierarchy, but his reign of fifty years brought peace and prosperity. He was succeeded by his eldest son with the title of Jehangir, the 'World-grasper', and he was followed by Shahjehan the 'Ruler of the World', and finally by Aurungzebe, the last of the great Moguls, whose title was Alamgir the 'World holder'. They are great names these titles of the Moguls who succeeded Akbar, Jehangir, Shahjehan, Alumgir, the sonorous Persian descriptives that sing themselves as they go, and these four great reigns which lasted from the days of English Elizabeth to those of Anne, were days of immense power wealth and prestige. The Empire ran from the Oxus down almost to Cape Comorin before it fell. Aurungzebe, for he is more usually known by his name than by his title Alamgir, conquered with want of foresight the Moslem kingdoms of the south, thus opening a way for a Hindu power in the south-west to raise its head. The first two successors to Akbar did display reasonable consideration for their Hindu subjects and wove them into the structure of Empire. Aurungzebe was far different. The old fanaticism of Islam had seized him. He re-introduced the almost forgotten *jiziah*, the poll tax on non-Moslems. He dominated because he was a man of iron will, and had tools to his hands, but when he was gone the whole structure slowly toppled by its own weight. When it fell the crash and the debris were immense, and it was pieces of this great crashed dominion that the British have steadily been piecing together these last two hundred years.

It is often said that this crash was due to the recovery of the Hinduism of the land, but though the Mahrathas, that half-bred race supported by the most intellectual Brahmin clans that ever gained ascendancy in India were a rising power, yet Mahrathadom so built its faith on spoliation, that it cannot be regarded as a national movement. Nevertheless Mahrathadom and Sikhism like the ivy on the wall did undoubtedly largely undermine the Mogul structure which was so weak in the consistence of its own cement. What Hinduism and Brahminism could have effected had not the British power fallen into the guardianship it is impossible to say. Certainly no homogeneous dominion could have arisen, in a continent so diversely composed.

The Shiah Story

In discussing Islam to which power temporal is so essential, political history has of necessity been included. It cannot be excluded in discussing Brahminism and its popular form Hinduism, which can flourish under a British Crown, but could come to no fruition so long as they were under the heel of a central Moslem dynasty. The Akbars are few in the world's story and their ends rarely comparable with their deserts.

Before leaving this outline of Islam both in the world and in India, it is necessary to say something more of Shi-ism, the other branch which broke off from central Islam over the difficult matter of the succession. The *rafzis*, or heretics, as the orthodox call the Shiahs, grew and developed in the countries under the Caliphs, but power temporal was denied them. After Ali, the Ommayad dynasty of the Caliphs flourished and completed the Arab Empire from its centre at Damascus. In the year 750, as related, the last of the Ommayads was killed, and Abul-Abbas founded the Abbassid line of Caliphs which endured in glory and in humiliation for five hundred years. It made its centre at Baghdad, since the Eastern move of the Empire called for a capital of eastern access. Baghdad was but Babylon and Seleucia in more modern form, the place on the Tigris or adjacent Euphrates where river-borne traffic must take to pack. Because of its economic and strategic position, Baghdad as the centre of this mighty Moslem Empire grew in power and might. And it is to be remembered that the Caliph, so long as he was really Caliph, was the titular head of all Islam temporal. To him all such Moslem conquerors as Mahmud of Ghuzni reported their conquests and made allegiance. It was not till the Baghdad Empire faded into the hands of Seljuk Turks, that there were none so poor as did them reverence.

The essential difference between Shiah and Sunni is this. It is not only the matter of the succession that was in question but the divinity, almost the incarnation of the Prophet and his family, as being in reality far more than a leader and a teacher, something deeper than *Rasul il Illah*, the Prophet of God. Ali and his descendants the Twelve Imams, which included Hassan and Hussayn, were not merely 'successor' to the Prophet in the power temporal, but the incarnate leaders of the faithful. The bulk of Shiah-dom believe that the Twelfth Imam, a boy, Muhammad Ibn Hasan-El-Askari, 'Muhammad the son of Hasan the Soldier' disappeared mysteriously while pitifully searching for his lost father in a cave at Samara, seventy miles north of Baghdad, to reappear as *Al Mahdi* the 'Guide', for whom indeed all Islam also looks. These are known as the 'Twelvers', and pending the arrival of *Al Mahdi*, the Shah of Persia is recognised as his representative and *locum tenens* here on earth. But there is a considerable division of the Shiahs known as the Ismailis, and also the Druses of the Lebanon, who consider Ismail the eldest son of the Sixth Imam, Jaafar es Saidik, as the last of the Imams to be present with the faithful here on earth. They are popularly known as 'the Seveners'. The Druses are a body who have initiates and secret cults and beliefs which centre round the Seventh Imam, but except in this point are not identical with the Ismailis or 'Seveners'.

Under the Abbassids, the followers of Ali lived their lives developed their new mysticism, and recognized as their spiritual head the elected descendant of Ali, and ere long were divided into two main divisions. When the Persian rose to might on the decay of Baghdad, then Shi-ism had a powerful temporal head. Holy places of the Shiahs are Kerbela and Nejef in Mesopotamia, and there not only countless Shiahs go in pilgrimage, but the bodies of thousands are brought to be buried near the burial place of Hussayn, where high prices are paid to this day for burial sites close to the precincts. In Iraq, the major portion of the Arab tribes south of Baghdad, belong to the Shiah sect, while those to the North are Sunni. The King of Iraq, King Feisal, one of the family of the former Shereef of Mecca, is of course orthodox, and as such perhaps not too well equipped to rule over the tribes of the hostile dispensation. During the British provisional occupation and government of the country, the Shiahs who in Basra were in great numerical superiority, were for the first time for centuries, administered in accordance with the Shiah as distinct from the orthodox Moslem law, a proceeding which they greatly appreciated.

The Ismailis

The Ismailis were and no doubt in some sense are a secret cult also, and they flourished in Persia and Syria from the eleventh to the thirteenth century. The founder, Hasan-ibn-Sabbah, seized, in the year 1070, the fortress of Alamut in Persia, where he established a society consisting of a supreme ruler, the *Sheikh el Jebel*, with three grand priors, priors or *rafiks*, and the companions or *fedawis*. European historians have named the head, the Sheikh el Jebel, the 'Old Man of the Mountains'. For some strange reason, their chief cult was the ridding of the world of prominent people, possibly on the grounds held elsewhere that all leaders are oppressors of mankind or of religions! The removal was carried out by the companions of the *fedawis* or 'faithful ones', after having

The Domes and Minarets of Islam
The "Taj Mahal" at Agra

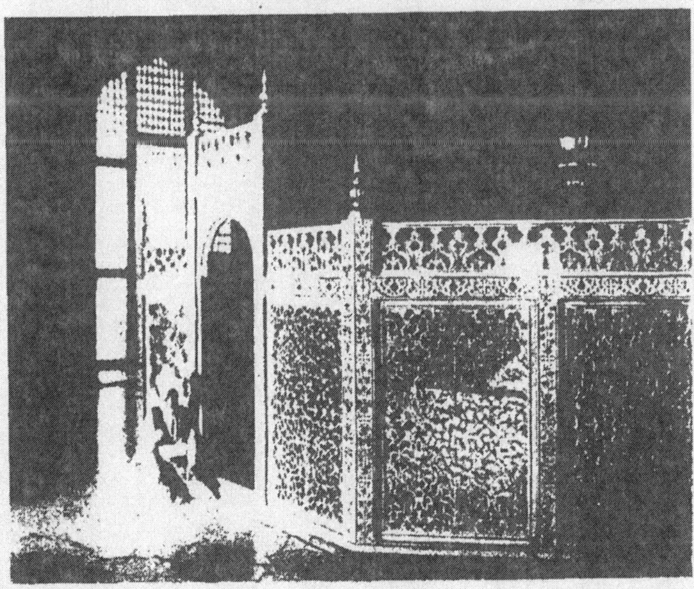

Fretted Marble Screen at the Taj Mahal

been intoxicated with *hashish*, and they were thus known as the *Hashishins* or 'hemp-eaters' corrupted in Crusading times to 'Assassin' whence the present English word for planned murderer. The last 'Old Man of the Mountains' was Rukhn ud Din, and they were expelled from Persia by the Mongols under Hulagu, in 1266, when twelve thousand were put to death. Two crusading leaders perished under their daggers, Raymond of Tripoli and Conrad of Montserat. A section in the Lebanon has developed into the Druses as explained above.

This description has been given at some length, because a portion of the Assassins escaped to India, where they have developed into a wealthy trading fraternity known generally as the Khojas or 'worthy men'. The descendant of, or successor to the Old Man of the Mountains, and head at any rate of the mystical cult of the Ismailis, is none other than the owner of a Derby winner, the 'Agha Khan', whose ancestor, a wanderer in Baluchistan during Sir Charles Napier's conquest of and command in Sind, was given shelter and protection and became a resident in Bombay. The Agha Khan is the recipient of the tribute of the faithful both from the wealthy Khojahs, and it is said from so far afield as Syria and the Jebel Druse, in his position as the recognized leader and Prince Palatine of the sect. But it will be realized that he is not an authority in the world of orthodox Islam or in the greater Shiah-dom. His real influence in his knowledge as a man of the world, and to his supreme importance to the British man in the street as being a keen patron of a popular British sport, and above all as the owner of a Derby winner. So far as the cult of the Ismailis go it is to mystical side of their worship and belief in Allah that interest attaches, and to their position as a secret cult whose real side as that of all Shiahs, is not fully explained to a curious world.

The Moslem Canon

The Hindu Canon has been outlined, and that of Islam, ruling as it does from sixty to seventy million Indians, is equally germane to this story. There is but one Moslem gospel, *Al Qoran*,[1] but as in the Christian Canon, nothing was left in writing by the Teacher. When the Prophet had gone, then it was that those in touch with him tried to remember and record what he taught. As were the Hindu sacred books handed down by word of mouth for centuries without gloss of copyist, so must the sayings of Muhammad, like the sayings of Christ, have been faithfully and accurately transmitted by that world of good memories. The Qoran like the Pentateuch contains not only gospel and theology but also law. The law of the Qoran written for a desert folk was soon inadequate for a world dominion, and hence grew up from the hands of Moslem leaders and lawgivers the '*Sunnat*' (the traditional law). The *Sunnat* is the interpretations of the Prophet and his successors, of the divine law, as revealed by Gabriel to the Prophet, and recorded later in the Qoran. Added to the *Sunnat* is the '*Ijma*', the dicta of the fathers of the faithful on any points obscure in the Qoran or the *Sunnat*. Lastly come the '*Kias*', reasons and deductions made by the learned from the injunctions and decisions of the other three.

These four works the *Qoran*, the *Sunnat*, the *Ijma* and the *Kias* form the Moslem Canon. Of Moslem writings and learned works, as in all other religions of thoughtful or educated men, there are legion, but these four at the Canon. They are written in Arabic, and as in the case of Latin, much is learnt by heart by those who understand not at all. For instance many of the fierce frontier mullahs

[1] Note:—There are two "K's" in Arabic, and it is the modern custom to express the more guttural one by "q".

of a scene, such as depicted in the first chapter, have not the slightest real knowledge of the language in which they spout their texts.

Arabic is *par excellence* the language of Islam. And assuredly it is the language of the devout. The phrases of such are on all men's lips, whether meant or customary. '*Inshallah*', 'Please God', is the tag with which every Moslem will end his statement of wishes or intentions. As beautiful as our Good-bye is the Arabic farewell, '*Fi Aman Ullah*', 'Go in the peace of God', 'In God's name', '*B'ism Illah*' is of frequent use, and many more. The name of the Almighty is always on a Moslem's lips and often in his thoughts. The Moslem tells his thirty-three beads, and repeats the ninety-and-nine attributes of God, The All-wise, the All-seeing, the All-merciful and so forth. The hundredth attribute is not known of the uninitiated, and men say that it is the same as the *Shem Hamephorash* of the Hebrew, the 'Ineffable Name'. The desert will tell you that the camel knows and therefore looks so scornful, and further that the word is akin to the lost word of the Master-mason. The *Sunnat* of the Shiahs often differs from that of the Orthodox, and often the Sunnis force the Shiahs to use their version. It is to be remembered that the Qoran claims to provide for all law, and there is no secular law in Islamic countries as the West understands it.

Mysticism in Islam

The ordinary practice of orthodox Islam cannot be said to have any great mystical inclination, and desire for oneness with the Deity. Severely monotheistic, and theoretically submissive to the Almighty, yes, but desirous of close communion no, although as we see in all religion, modern expounders are tending to develop a more spiritual teaching. Yet the heart of man seems to have that craving, in all countries and in all climes, and the Shiah division of Islam undoubtedly does present a more mystical side to its adherents. Not only has the leader disappeared from earth, but his return as *Al Mahdi*, who shall put the world right, is confidently awaited, whether it be the Twelfth Imam of the 'Twelvers', or the Seventh Imama of the 'Seveners', who has passed away from sight to come again, the principle is the same, there is to come some prophet or person who shall bring man to God, and put the World right. Indeed all Islam looks for the Mahdi.[1] Shiahdom points how and who.

But this demand for mystic communion in Islam has been to some extent satisfied in a sect or society that is both ancient and modern. The Sufis, for Sufi-ism is a Moslem mystical cult, theoretically open to the world, are actually confined to the followers of the Prophet. Sufi-ism was a revolt against the rigid law and wearisome Moslem ritual of Persia. It eventually crystallized into a pantheistic mysticism tinted with the teachings of ancient Zoroaster adopting a theory of life not far removed from Buddhism. But while the Buddhist seeks release to contemplation and renunciation, the Sufi seeks a growing acquaintance with God, that shall culminate in ecstatic adoration, and a love which will dispel all inferior affections. Sufis will be found far and wide in Moslem countries, and among devout Moslems many Sufis will be encountered in India, by he who sets himself out to meet them. Indeed the European who will frequent the byways and eschew the beaten path, will find many a Sufi ready to exchange greetings and signs and welcome one who speaks with tongues and understanding to the initiated—and Sufis

[1] The uprising of a local false *mahdi* in the Sudan will be well remembered in Britain.

will contend that only by initiation and a long period of approbation and trial can full Sufi-ism be attained. The final state is reached by five stages, *Service* . . obedience to the will of God . . *Love* . . that is to say the attraction of the soul to God . . *Seclusion* . . which implies meditation on things divine . . *Knowledge* . . only acquired by metaphysical studies of the character and attributes of the Godhead, and fifthly *Ecstasy* . . the excited state reached by means of a full comprehension of the love and power of God. The Sufi contends that the uninitiated cannot even attempt to understand what these five degrees of the cult really imply. Sufism is said to have inspired the best of Persian poetry.

The Orthodox Schools and Sects[1]

Within Moslem Orthodoxy there are several sects which we should call schools. Some represent but views as to law and some represent more modern views of doctrine, predestination, freewill, etc., but are admissible schools of thought without incurring the tint of a heresy that must be hunted. There has even been from very early times a rationalist school, which was not disposed to accept the Qoran, compiled by man even if from the memory of inspired utterances and teachings, as being necessarily correctly remembered, interpreted, or even copied. The rationalists in older times were persecuted, save in the days of the Caliph Mamun, who had similar views himself.

But the sect that really is important both religiously and politically is that of the Wahabis, a perfectly orthodox, and militantly Puritan sect, founded by an Arab Abdul Wahab who lived from 1691 to 1765. Intense hostility to any laxity of life, to any giving way to so-called pleasures,

[1] Some notes on modern sects are given in Chapter IX.

to any neglect of the austerities of the Moslem rule of life. The spirit of John Knox and of Cameron, and the dourer covenanters was theirs. In 1803 having a large following they over rode parts of Arabia captured Mecca and threatened Egypt. Turkey through Egypt invaded Arabia and crushed the movement, but as the Puritan movement of Islam it has considerable influence and power, lurking in the potholes of the Arabian desert and flaring forth. The world has lately seen the remarkable recrudescence when Ibn Saud, Chief of Nejed in the Arabian desert near the Persian Gulf, has led the Wahabi followers to seize Mecca once again, from the somewhat ineffective and difficult family of Sherif Hussayn of Mecca, and the Moslem world has acquiesced in the casting out of the money-changers and the cleansing of the temple involved. The force in Arabia is the Wahabi *Ikhwan*, or 'brothers' who embody all that is dour and fierce and austere in the Arab complex. Wahabis flourish in the Muhammedan city of Patna, which now exists on the famous old Hindu capital of Magadha that was Paliputra. Fierce in their enmity against slackness, the British at times incur the enmity which lashes their own weaker brethren, and they have had their share in stimulating the troubles on the Afghan border. Alfred Lyall, that wonderful interpreter of the East, makes a fierce Arab Wahabi say to the Moslem of India

> Men of the Indian cities who call on the Prophet's name
> By our brotherhood in Islam ye besought me, and I came
> From a country hard and barren, to a softly watered land
> To a round sky line of harvest from a wilderness of sand

and then he rails on them, the man of the moss-hags,

> From our bare and barren homesteads from our feasts of
> dates and milk
> To your palaces, your fleshpots and your raiment of silk.

The Juma Masjid at Lahore

The Juma Masjid at Delhi
Stately Islam

[*Face page* 102

But he finds them too soft to his purpose, and can only lead them—

> When ye shun the Hindu festivals the tinkling of the
> bell,
> The dancing, the idolatries, the harlotry of hell—

and so on and so forth as John Knox to Mary Stuart.

Islam and Christianity

It is customary to believe that there is an unbridgeable gulf between Islam and Christianity, that can never be spanned, and though the past has shown that this bitterness and enmity can exist, there is reason for it, not inherent in the faiths. The Prophet is said by some to have had a Jewish and by other traditions a Christian mother. But as both these religions were fairly dispersed in Western Asia, it may well have been so. The rule of life of Islam is devout and especially punctilious in its outward observance of the rules for worship. The outward carelessness of the Western Christian is somewhat a scandal in Moslem eyes, and the Christian in the East does often undoubtedly fail to give his own Church a fair chance to earn Moslem good opinion.

Only in the most ignorant of circles can a Christian be known by the term for those outside the pale, that is *Kafir* ('unbeliever'). To the Moslem, Christian and Jew are '*Ahl-i-kitab*' ('People of the Book'), people who base their rule of life and daily action on a divinely revealed Scripture. The enmity between Christian and Moslem of the past is undoubtedly the legacy of the Crusades, and of the political as distinct from the religious aspect thereof.

More than once does the Prophet Muhammad say in the *suras* . . i.e. the chapters of the Qoran, that Jesus is truly the son of God,[1] and that Miriam is his mother. Again does he tell his followers that 'the Christians are your friend, and the Jews your enemies'. This the result of the attitude of the Jews in Arabia at the time of the persecution of Muhammad by the Arabs before the Hijra, especially certain Arabs converted to Judaism.

It is even possible for Christians to believe that the prophet Muhammad was truly a Prophet sent of God to a people who would not accept Christianity or were not yet ready for Christianity, and further that there are some races and peoples so undeveloped that Islam is a fitting half-way house of development for those who may ultimately become Christians. To entertain the possibility of this idea it is necessary to understand time and what it means. Christianity did not become a world religion till centuries after Christ, Buddhism took many hundred years to develop and spread. It is at any rate perfectly practicable for Christianity and Islam to live side by side in God's good purpose. But both are missionary religions. Christianity has what the Duke of Wellington once said to an officer, who objected to missions, its "marching orders," to spread the Gospel. Islam at the present moment, eager to establish itself in the modern world's eyes, also is active in the mission field, and is competing with Christianity for conversion in Africa, as well as to prevent any reversion to Hinduism in India.

Because the world is on the whole a peaceful world, the old carrying of the faith at the sword's point has passed away, and the Moslem missionary must depend on the appeal of his teaching. To the negroid folk of inner

[1]Moslems however contend that the Arabic means 'spirit' of God rather than 'son' accepting the divine origin of the conception. When El Mahdi appears he will establish Christ's rule on earth.

Africa, it does bring such an amelioration of hope and outlook, as to be an uplift and a promise. Compared with Christianity it also brings a less-cabined rule of life to a backward people. It has already been explained that in the conquest of India by Islam in the past, it did bring vast hope of moral and social uplift and status to the aboriginal folk that the contemptuous Aryan cast out, and also came as breath of fresh air to Aryans themselves, clogged with the lush and futile forms and ceremonies of popular Hinduism.

In modern times the more scientific prosecutor of Christian missionary enterprise, well recognizes this aspect of Islam, and would gladly be understood of and understand Moslem outlook, leaving it to the Almighty to direct the trend of conversion, and to know which man cannot, how far Islam is working with a blessing. It is also to be remembered that Islam is by no means an unchanging faith. Its educated outlook varies in many parts of the world, and through the centuries, the teaching tends to develop as in the case of other religions and even of Christianity. The orthodox Muhammadan does find the need for the more mystical teaching which the Shiahs in some sense undoubtedly have. For the chief criticism that the world as a whole can make of Islam, is the thinness of the appeal to the deeper mind.[1]

[1] The Modern sects within the orthodox pale and the Great Moslem festivals will be discussed in Chapter IX.

CHAPTER VI

THE FANCY RELIGIONS OF INDIA

THE FANCY RELIGIONS OF INDIA—CHRISTIANITY, IN EARLY TIMES—THE PARSEES—SIKHISM—THE JEWS IN INDIA—ANIMISTS.

THE FANCY RELIGIONS OF INDIA

BECAUSE the stock established religions of India are Hinduism (including Brahminism) and Islam, I have used the old sergeant-major's term for the numerically lesser creeds, including so far as its history goes Christianity in this more profane category. "Church of England to the right, fancy religions to the left" was the old order, or its alternative of the Sunday parade, "Column of Superstitions in rear of the Established Church". These Fancy Religions gathered thus together for the sake of making a full chapter, are Christianity, the oldest of them all in India, if the 'respectable' story of St. Thomas at the Mount and his sojourn with Gondophares in the north be true; Parseeism, the ancient faith of Zoroaster, and that of what has been called 'those eternal contemporaries', the Jews, which is the story of the very early phase of the dispersion, and Sikhism which is a story by itself, although an offshoot of Hinduism.

Buddhism has been dealt with at greater length, and a Jainism at lesser length, and are outside the category of fancy religions for our purpose, but within may properly be described the Animism of the wilder Indian tribes, and that extraordinarily interesting phenomenon, the spirit worship of the hill-tribes in Burma, so especially of value as possibly throwing great light by seeing before us to-day the working of the human mind in the evolution of religion from its very beginning. Unfortunately the touch of the West comes so very quickly now to the East that in a very few years the simplicity and authenticity of origin will be gone, and impressions must be taken now lest they fade.

Christianity in Early Times.

Christianity in India is no new thing. Long before the return of that country to Hinduism and Brahminism, after the sojourn in the wilderness of that joint and several creed, Christianity had come to India. There is this legend of Gondophares, the Parthian, receiving a mission under the leadership of Saint Thomas which is in no way improbable, while there is the strong belief, which is not quite susceptible of proof, that the ancient Christian settlement of St. Thomas's Mount in Madras was really established by the Apostle himself, who is said to have eventually suffered a martyrdom near Madras.

That settlement has long been part of the Church of the East *par excellence*, to which Rome in contempt gave the name Nestorian, and which is really the Catholic Church of Assyria, and was once the Church of Persia, and even of China. Before the Uniate Church, known as the Chaldæan Church, broke off from the Assyrian Matrix, of which Nestorius was once Bishop, and which being outside the Roman Empire did not go to Nicæa, the fraternity of St. Thomas Mount was formed, and being almost beyond the reach of any fierce Moslem movement, had no difficulty in surviving. About the fifth century it put itself under the jurisdiction of the (Syrian) Patriarch at Mosul.[1] It has several branches, one being united with Rome and thus in modern parlance the 'Syrian' Church proper. The coming of Portugal and the missions of St. Francis Xavier did produce a very considerable spread of Christianity into Western India.

At the beginning of the sixteenth century the Portuguese had succeeded in establishing themselves on the West Coast of India, not as merchants under treaty, as the English were to do, but by sheer invasion, accompanied by some astounding acts of massacre and cruelty on the high seas if their own historians are to be believed. The romance of Vasco da Gama's enterprise in first reaching India at the end of the fifteenth century was much tarnished by these subsequent actions, which, however, led to the conquest of a certain amount of country belonging to the Zamorin of Calicut, and the establishment of what, had there been enough of the true enterprising race in the make-up, should have been an Empire of the East. The successive Armadas, which national enterprise now sent regularly to support the earlier successes, need not be entered into here, nor the operations, invasions and piracies which the Portuguese undertook in their conception of making the Indian Ocean as far as Aden and the Persian Gulf, Portuguese waters. With their land-Empire came the Church of Rome, with a magnificent enterprise with which history connects the name of St. Francis Xavier, also to be greatly tarnished later by the operations of an Inquisition, which for generations made the name of Christian execrated in Western India. Nevertheless, large numbers of Indians were baptized in the years

[1] Mosul is the modern Nineveh.

between 1500 and 1600. The Inquisition under the Dominicans was introduced in 1560.[1]

Goa itself has long been the centre of the Church of Rome in India, from which centre firmly established, and in the midst of a largely Christian people, it speaks with more authority than from any other part of India.

But Portuguese India fell from its high estate after over two centuries of rule. It never recovered the siege and capture of Bassein by the Mahrathas, and that town of ruined churches and spires, shows how an earnest Christian rule could establish itself. The union of Portugal with Spain was the real cause, however, of the dimunition of her Empire of the East. Her resources were swept into the bigger and more embarrassing future of South America, and concentration on India and the Gulf ceased. A century after the Portuguese dominion commenced, the British merchant-adventurers with their charter arrived, and had not the least intention of putting up with any rough ways at sea from the Portuguese, with the result that events were slowly leading up towards the loss of Bassein, close to that wonderful dowry of Bombay which came with the bride of Charles II.

The people of the Goa province had largely embraced Christianity, and to this day are to be found all over India in clerical, domestic and musician employment. Though their names are the high sounding ones of the old Portuguese families, the descendants of the actual officers and men who married Indian women, are far fewer than the actual Indians themselves, who adopted on baptism the name of the Governor of their province or other high functionary. In British India it is believed that many of the earlier Christians took names from

[1] The records of eleven *Auta da fé* include one hundred and twenty one burnings.

the tombstones in the European cemeteries. Neither method therefore gives clue to descent.

Jesuit missionaries were at the Mogul court so early as 1580, in the days of the broad-minded and enquiring Akbar, and Christian chapels existed at Agra, Delhi and Lahore, though these are believed to have disappeared in the days of the bigoted Aurungzebe Alamgir.

Some references have been made to obscure sects with some Christian traces of old time conversions and teachings. Mahabharak, writing three hundred years after Christ, refers to the visit of three saints from a white country, teaching a perfect *bhakti*. Some of the passages referred to must have been taken from St. John, and the term *maha-prasad* used means 'sacramental.'

But Christianity, other than as recorded, came to India seriously as a matter of missionary activities in the end of the eighteenth century, with the Dutch and Danish, and then the British missionary activities. The East India Company was very naturally anxious to 'go slow,' for the whole of its political influence might have fallen had a religious hostility been engendered and activity misunderstood. It was not till the days of Lord William Bentinck, in the years immediately before the Victorian era, that the great start was made, under famous missionaries, to which incidentally the whole fabric of education in Bengal and through Bengal, Northern India owes so much of its encouragement. The astounding move towards Christianity among the humble of the Dravidian races during the last quarter of a century will be outlined later.

THE PARSEES

The Parsees or Parsis, which is another form of the word, Farsi, inhabitants of Fars, or Persia, are one of the most interesting peoples in India. It is the custom to consider them as not part and parcel of India, and yet they have been longer in the land than any of the Tartar or Afghan colonists that are recognizable as such. Yet in truth they are not of India, having retained with the intensity of the Jews, their racial and religious aloofness. They are of special interest too, and in India as representing perhaps the Aryan race at its purest, and still practising the ancient religion of Aryan Persia as taught by Zoroaster in Achaemenian times, and using in their sacred writings of the Zend-Avesta, the ancient religious book of Persia, written in what is sometimes probably erroneously known as the '*Zend.*'

The Parsis first came to Din in Kathiawar, no doubt as merchants and traders, so far back as A.D. 75, moving to Sanjan on the coast of Guzerat, nineteen years later. They must have remained in Guzerat many centuries, increasing their settlement for business purposes, but only existing as sojourners, reinforced by drafts of friends and relatives from Persia. But in A.D. 640 when the Caliph Omar and his fierce proselytizing Arabs invaded Persia, those of the old race who would not accept Islam, fled from their native land and came to India, the land of their trading settlements. With the fall of Yazedgird, the last of the Sassanian kings before the invaders, the old Persian Empire was gone, and these Persians adopted this date of their flight as the first year of the calendar of their exile, as Muhammad had adopted the date of his flight or *hijra* for his year one.

We do not know very much of the Parsis' history during the many centuries succeeding their exodus, save that as wealthy, and with-all amenable and kindly traders they were accepted both by the Hindu and Moslem rulers of India. It was not not till so late as 1640 that they came to what is now their main habitat, the Islands of Bombay, about the time that the latter came to Charles II as the thrice eventful dowry of Catherine of Braganza, his bride. But since those days with all the stimulus of British trade and British protection they have become a people of astounding wealth. They still number less than a million, but have always so managed their social grading that never has a depressed or inferior class arisen. All except the constitutionally worthless are woven into a prosperous community. As men of learning and science they are not unknown in the high places of the world. Their women are more than comely, and their old men have often the most handsome features of a type usually associated with the Western Aryan, though curiously enough the beauty of their women is of a more Semitic type.

Besides the *Zend Avesta*, the sacred books of the Parsees in modern use are:

The Yesna—a Text of Ritual,
The *Visperea*—a liturgical appendix to the Yasna,
The *Venidad*—the priestly code,
The *Yashio*—Song of Praise,
Khonda-avesta.

Not very much is known of Zarathrusthra, which is popularly written Zoroaster, but he is said to have been like Gautama, of princely origin, who set himself to reclaim the Persians from wild unholy paganism some eight hundred years before Christ. His tenets and lessons however are believed to be as now practised by the Parsees from the *Zend Avesta*, aforesaid, and a more popular code of morals deduced therefrom in the Revelations of the *Arda Viraj*. It was much a protest against the license and idolatry of the age as was that of Muhammad to the folk of Arabia thirteen hundred years later. The monotheism is expressed much as in the *Kalima* of the Prophet, "There is only one God and no other is to be compared to him", and with the attributes ascribed to Eloihim, or Jahweh, in the Old Testament. As all explainers of life have done, Zoroaster taught that there were two agencies, that of good and evil ever in conflict. Ahura-Mazdao (the 'wise Lord'), more often spoken of by the contracted form of Ormuzd, is the Parsee name of the Almighty, Ahriman, the spirit of evil. Lesser godlets and Devas or spirits figured in the original teaching, but modern Parsee thought has eliminated all such, and is a severe monotheism. The priests are a hereditary class and are born to the robe and duty. The rule of life of Zoroastrians is summed up in a very few words.

"Perform good actions and refrain from evil ones." Ever is the spirit warring with the flesh. There was no blending of the human soul with the Divine *Atman*, and no reconciliation of man's suffering with God's law. The souls of the dead pass over the "Accountant's Bridge" before admission to the spiritual world. The descriptions of heaven and hell might be taken from the vision of the prophets and from St. John. But the principal attributes of the Zoroastrian, as they are to the Parsees to this day, are philosophy, benevolence and philanthropy. Zoroaster never seemed to have sought proselytes, nor do modern Parsees. His followers are also known as 'Fire-worshippers,' fire and light appertaining to the good agency in the world, and dead embers and darkness the evil. The sacred fire to this day is a feature in Parsee places of worship, and is indeed a powerful emblem of the eternal. The method adopted by Parsees of the disposal of the dead always appears remarkable to others.

It is based on the idea that the sacred earth, the mother of life and foodstuffs, must not be polluted by anything dead and decaying, an idea also no doubt behind the Hindu burning of the dead. The Parsee corpse is placed without covering on the top of a high tower on a grating. Torn by the birds of the air, the bones stripped of flesh fall to the charnel house below, in what are known as the 'Towers of Silence,' usually erected in some isolated rising ground.

Sikhism

The inclusion of Sikhism in this chapter of 'Fancy' religions, is partly for convenience, but only partly so, for though modern Hindu thought does want, and affect, to include Sikhism as among its side shows, yet it is in essence far otherwise. It is true that most of its members were originally drawn from Hindu races, and that as the rose would return to the briar, everything that has left it tends to return to it. Brahminism has succeeded in permeating the Sikh mind or the educated Sikh mind almost unknown to it, yet Sikhism is emphatically a thing apart. In the first chapter of this book an outline of the rise of *Baba* Nanak, one of the many reformers, and probably a follower and admirer of the great Kabir, has been given.

The sixteenth century was a very active period in religious thought and searchings in that world, the mediæval power of Rome in the West was breaking, and as has been said, it was about the time of Martin Luther that Baba Nanak began to teach. It will be noticeable, even in this short outline of the rise and wane and resurrection of Hinduism, how constant has been the stream of reformers, endeavouring to extract some gripping rule of life, out of the tropical emanations from obscure Vedic principles, Aryan imaginations and Dravidian fears.

Kabir-Panthis (Followers of Kabir) at Prayer

For the few that are on record, and the still fewer whose names have been mentioned here, there have been thousands whose names have gone out, or may be obscurely recorded in some quiet little mountain or jungle pocket. Why the teachings of one more than another 'caught on' is hard to say. Why Gautama should have led the millions and Mahavira only the thousands, is hard to explain, nor the fact that Buddhism having swept the land for centuries and died while the sect of Mahavira the Jinna still remains. It will be noted too, how most of the reformers take something of the same line; they endeavour to concentrate thought on the Supreme behind all lesser conceptions, they all teach the simple kindly life, some would find salvation by works and some by faith. The Grace and Salvation teachings have been many, and those within the Hindu fold have brought a way of peace to countless thousands.

Among then the rising and falling of reformers, it is not easy to say why Sikhism should have remained when the Kabirpanthis for instance are but a handful. But the reason probably lies in the story of the oppression by the Moguls that produced the Tenth Guru, and perhaps in the fact that the teaching was calculated to flourish in the sturdiness of the particular race among whom it incubated, the Jāts between Delhi and the Ravi River. The cruel execution of the Ninth Guru set the seal of success to Sikhism, and gives one more point to Talleyrand's remark to the young man who propounded his new religion, "It is a fine religion but . . . to start it you must be crucified."

The Sikhs have bulked very large in Indian history of late years, partly because of the two severe wars in the early days of Queen Victoria's reign. These eventuated in the Punjab province being re-united by the British to the dominions of the Great Mogul, from which Ahmad Shah the founder of the Afghan Empire had broken them off. In referring to these wars it is to be remembered that the first was due to the fierce era of murder, indiscipline and debauchery that followed on the death of the only Sikh king, Ranjhit Singh, the Sikh government to save itself, precipitating its own unruly army onto the British as the lesser evil. The British were anxious to preserve this buffer kingdom between themselves and the Afghan power. They, therefore, after smashing the rebellious army, tried to restart the Sikh state with the putative heir, little Dhulip Singh on the throne, under tutelage. But the restless Sikh element, a very small one in a great Moslem province, would not abide by the decision. The old Sikh mercenary soldier wanted another try for his prestige. Several conflicting elements produced the rebellion against Dhulip Singh's government, and the fierce battles of the Second Sikh War followed with the crowning victory of Goojerat to Lord Gough's army. In a province of some twenty millions there are now little over two million Sikhs, the total of the whole people, women and children included, is but three million even now. Of these close on a million live south of the Sutlej and the Punjab proper, in what used to be called the 'protected' Sikh states. These were Sikh states in existence when the British came to Delhi, at the beginning of the nineteenth century, and which the British undertook to protect from the devouring maw of the young moss-trooping chief who was making a Punjab kingdom for himself out the Afghan provinces.

The great zeal with which Sikhs and Moslems of the Punjab, enthusiastically pro-British under the Lawrence traditions, flocked down to destroy the Muhammadan pretenders and the Bengal sepoy in the Mutiny at Delhi and Lucknow, and their distinguished service in the post-Mutiny Army has brought the Sikhs into greater prominence than their numbers quite warrant. Their leaders are well aware of this, and have shown it in their very proper demand for a sufficient representation in the Punjab Parliament to protect their interests from their many enemies. So much for their political position at the present day. Sikhs are a religious community, and not a racial one. But, in that the religion has principally flourished among that portion of the Jăt race that inhabit the Punjab. Sikhism is in many ways the religion of the Punjab Jăts. There are however also Hindu and Moslem Jăts in the Punjab, while south of the Punjab, the race calling themselves Jăts is chiefly Hindu. The Jăt race and its interesting story are outside the province of this book, save that it may here be mentioned that through the ages they have not been admitted in public, and Brahmin opinion as a race entitled to consider itself Rajput, i.e. descendants of princes. But social uplift has always bulked big in any Indian people's complex. It has been suggested to the Jăts by emissaries of the political wing of the Arya Samaj, that an abandonment of their traditional British loyalty might be rewarded by a re-examination in a favourable light of their desire to be called Rajputs, which is perhaps but another chapter of the 'Book of Snobs'.

Baba Nanak, who lived from 1469 to 1539, was a member of the Khatri caste, therefore a high caste Hindu, and was born and brought up on the banks of the Ravi near Lahore. After being married and having sons, he turned mendicant, affecting the society of Sadhus, with whom he travelled far and wide, and visited most of the famous places of pilgrimage. Tradition says that he even went as far afield as Mecca. He was an ordinary orthodox

Hindu, but was said to have picked up some of the ideas of the Sufis. Eventually he evolved his particular teaching, which aimed, like so many before him, on combining many faiths in the worship of the same god whom all under different guises revered. He taught the Creator-spirit, outside whom all is *maya*, illusion. Salvation could be attained through a Guru, a leader, as a mediator between God and man. Through the Guru, reincarnation could be avoided and *karma* defeated. It is thought that Nanak must in his wanderings, although there is no record extant, have come into considerable contact with Christian teaching, so much does Christian thought figure in his 'way'. Besides the Christians in Travancore, there is a sect of friars, or faqirs, claiming conversion by St. Thomas in the north, who have both the gospel of Matthew as well as the writings of Nanak. There is within the Granth the following—

> "As great as Thou thyself art, so great is thy gift.
> "Who having created the day, didst also create the night."

Many *sloks*, i.e. couplets in the Granth, have Christian affinities. In fact it has been said, from an examination of the Granth from certain aspects, that Nanak taught nothing but the story of Christ from Birth to Ascension.

There was nothing at all in Nanak's teaching and pretensions, to incur the enmity of any great rulers or religions, and his following should have been able to take the path of many other teachers of benevolence and piety. As has been mentioned, it is thought also that Nanak was inspired to take the rôle of teacher and reformer by the example and general teaching of Kabir. The Fifth Guru, Arjan, was an able man, who amassed some wealth and tried to blend the disciples into something of a race and a palatinate, and this first brought the sect into disfavour with the Moslem government. Arjan was probably put to death by the Moslems and his son Har Govindh succeeded him. In his hands the sect, hitherto a simple brotherhood began to take on military guise, and think about defending themselves. It was in the time of the Ninth Guru, Teg Bahadur 1664–75, that trouble really rose with authority, and the Emperor Aurungzebe who had so fiercely revived the almost dead practice of the persecution of non-Moslems, decided to exterminate the sect. The Guru was put to death with great cruelty and as already related, it was the rescue of his body by scavengers that brought license to the poor and humble to become disciples.

It was Guru Teg Bahadur, says tradition, who before his death, standing on the roof of his prison, told the Moguls "From the West will come my fair skinned disciples wearing helmets, who shall avenge my death and utterly destroy my enemies." This story is much quoted by the Sikhs themselves, and has by some been taken to account for their instinctive enthusiasm in the support of the British.

Teg Bahadur was succeeded by his son, Govindh, who from the age of fifteen years when his father died, brooded on that tragedy and the dispersion of the disciples. After much training and meditation he announced the appearance of a goddess (which we may, as already suggested, better interpret as a saint), who had directed an especial initiation and baptism into an austerer form of the brotherhood. This he forthwith inaugurated, the story of how does not matter here, the ceremony being known as 'taking the *Pahul*'. All the new disciples were to adopt the Rajput cognomen of Singh or 'Lion', and the Singhs were to be distinguished by the wearing of what is usually known as the 'Five' K's or *Kakkas* which are—

(1) The *Kes*, the uncut hair rolled in a knot on the head.
(2) The *Kachh*, a short drawers.
(3) The *Kirpan*, a steel dagger.
(4) The *Kara*, an iron bangle or quoit, a throwing missile.
(5) The *Kangh*, a small iron tooth comb, always worn in the hair.

Up to now the Nanakpanthis were but a Hindu sect, but the Tenth Guru had made their dress as distinctive as possible from Hindu or Moslem, and had now declaimed measures to separate them finally from any touch with that communion. Caste was abolished and the ranks of the brotherhood were thrown open to all comers, though unfortunately the caste instinct so deeply ingrained does still linger. The Jăts of the Punjab sturdy and quarrelsome, flocked to the new brotherhood, and he soon had a force which enabled him to try conclusions, though not always successfully with the forces at Delhi. He composed a code of law, the *Rahatnama*, for his Singhs, to be read in conjunction with the *Granth*.

Guru Govindh, says tradition, was murdered by a Pathan, in revenge, however, for his father's death at the Guru's hands. Before dying Govindh is reported to have said that no further Gurus were needed, and that he made over his brotherhood 'The *Khalsa*', or 'pure society', to God, and that henceforth the *Ad Granth* was to be the guide of his people. Therein he said would the Guru be found. It was thus three centuries after Baba Nanak taught, that Sikhism came into combined political and religious stability.

After this a bitter struggle between Sikh and Mogul continued, which contributed greatly to the downfall of the house of Timur.

The Sikh Canon is a small one. It consists of the two parts of the *Ad Granth*, the first, the *Japji* written by Baba Nanak, the second, explanations by subsequent Gurus of the extremely obscure, and often contradictory teachings of the *Japji*, and the *Daswin Badshahi*, or 'Tenth Government'. This was composed by Guru Govindh with a view to making his followers harder stuff that they would ever learn to be from the teachings of the *Japji*.

The teachings of the latter, confused though they are to follow, crystallize on the following—

> The Fatherhood of God and all that fatherhood means.
> The brotherhood of man.
> The necessity of obedience to the inward voice Divine.
> The unerring work of Divine justice.
> The necessity of a Divine Teacher
> The existence of a Mediator and Absolver of sin.
> The folly and evil of idolatry.

And these seven points show what a long way Sikhism had travelled from Hinduism with its complicated obsessions, and even from *Bhakti*. The law of the Singhs while embodying and accepting all these, are summed up so far as the warrior peasantry were concerned the faith as in these simple words.

> Accept one baptism.
> Worship one invisible God.
> Let 'Hail Teacher!' be their watchword.
> Of material things reverence steel alone.
> Be ever prepared for war, eager to die in the war.
> Maintain the five 'K's.'

In the precepts of Guru Govindh summarizing the *Japji*, it is written, a Sikh should set his heart on God and on the name of God, on Charity and Purity.

Worship God every day.
Keep a place in the heart for the poor.
Give a tithe of all possessions.
He who professes holiness should act as such.
Avoid the lustful eye.
Offend none, for the Lord's sake.
Look for the advent of a spotless incarnation.

Indeed may it be said that Guru saw the conclusion of the whole matter "Fear God and keep his commandments," and yet there are those who would maintain that Sikhism is a Hindu sect!

The matter of Sikhs in the Army and the British officer has been alluded to in Chapter I. Is it to be wondered that the British officers would foster such a faith among his soldiery?

There are a few sects among the Sikhs, of no great importance, the followers of certain teachers within orthodoxy. The most noted, however, is the military fanatical gang known as *Akalis* or *Nihangs*, so often to be met on the road in their blue clothes and high blue head-dresses, covered in quoits and the like, turbulent and insolent, but preserving Singhism. Maharajah Ranjhit Singh, to whom they were often insolent, gave them short shrift when they went too far, but put up with a lot from them.

There are certain movements among the Sikhs that are of great interest. The first is one, to get further away from Hinduism and range alongside Christianity, in admiration of the teaching of Christ. Another is to fall in with the endeavour of the Araya Samaj to rope them into the political fold of Hinduism.

A few years ago the brotherhood was very much torn over the question of temple lands. The attitude of the British to the religions of India, at all times tolerant and helpful, had confirmed at the time of the annexation, the rights of all religious bodies and the incumbents in the land of the temples. But temple grazing-lands that perhaps just kept the incumbent and his assistants a few years ago, may have become intensely valuable owing to the British bringing irrigation water. The priest-in-charge, the *mahant*, thus became wealthy. The congregations began a movement to segregate the lands for the good of the body. *Akalis*, ready for any fray, took part in demonstrations. The Government infuriated the people by giving police protection, saying the law must be maintained, and that if the Sikh fraternity as a whole wanted the position changed, let them propose an alteration of law. It was purely a Sikh matter, except so far as legal right went, and now happily adjusted, but it did create bitter disturbance, and as no ordinary Punjab mind could differentiate between private and government matters, the British got the odium.

The Jews in India

It is interesting to note that though the 'eternal contemporaries', the Jews, form but a very small community in India, they came as a colony in the remote ages, in one of the dispersions before the Christian Era. In Cochin there has been a settlement which consists of both 'Black' and 'White' Jews, which was, it is said, established two thousand years ago. Who or what the 'Blacks' are no man can say, whether they came in as converts with the whites, or whether some local Dravidian clan joined them as proselytes, as happened in so many places, neither history nor tradition says. Only the fact remains, but when we reflect on the conversions in the days of the Maccabees, on the origin of the Samaritans, or reflect how the 'flat-nosed' Jews of Russia are of Tartar origin, we shall see that there is nothing abnormal in what is presumably a non-Semite Jew. There are of course many Jewish merchants and traders domiciled in India for generations, or coming and going from Aden, or from those real homes of Jewry, Basra and Baghdad, and in Bombay, Poona and many other places there are enough to maintain handsome synagogues. The Jew in India, however, is of no special political account except that law and order is always his objective. The interest lies in the fact that they should be there at all. As elsewhere they make a contribution to mercantile pursuits in excess of their actual numbers, which in 1921 was but 22,000.

Animists

The Animists of India numbered close on ten million souls in the census of 1921. They have probably increased since then by another million on the general increase shown in the new census, of which the details have not yet been published, and comprise many different races, and are over and above those of Dravidian and aboriginal races to be classed as low caste Hindus. They comprise the more inaccessible jungle-folk living in the forest lands of Central India, the hills on the Madras coast of the Bay of Bengal, the Nilgerry hills, the hill tracts of Assam and Aracan, and people both of Negrito and very early Ruranian origin. Among them also are the Chins, Karens and Kachins of the Burmese hills, the latter including a strain of some higher race amid their usual Mongoloid stock, possibly from slave-taking in the past. Hovering in Burma itself, as has been referred to, is that strain of earlier Animistic cults which lies beneath the veneer of Burman Buddhism. The Animism of India may be classed into three divisions based on the historic fact that India was an Animistic country, in various stages of advancement, when the evolved Aryan religion began to absorb it.

The first group is that of the Animists entirely outside Hindu influence.

The second, those who have adopted some Hindu ways, are slightly civilized, but not recognized.

Thirdly, those who are in association with Hinduism, but are considered out-caste.

The objects of worship of the Animists are spirits of ancestors, rudimentary deities, and the forces of Nature. Within these three categories there is room for immense variety, both of hope and fear, custom and rite, good and evil. In all cases Animists are very much at the mercy of priests who may announce sudden instructions from gods and spirits, and who have, and do, introduce atrocious cults, especially where there is any natural desire for blood, as witness not only some of the cruelties of India, but such customs as head-hunting and human sacrifices among Chins, Was, and the like. Some of the beliefs and cults are simple enough, some shapeless god on the edge of a village, smeared with dung and paint, representing or calling to memory the village god. Others are dark and gloomy, demanding fierce and bloody sacrifices. Among the Kachins where the religious thought is simple and apparently kindly, the *Nats*, good, if capricious, spirits, presumably ancestors, are revered. Outside the village are places of worship where eggs are deposited, and which as the British soldier discovered in his campaigns are often fresh. The eggs are offered in receptacles of split bamboos of which the unsplit end is stuck in the ground.[1]

[1] Knowing something of Kachins, the writer having a Kachin battalion under his command in Mesopotamia, inquired when inspecting, if the Nats were pleased and thought well of the venture. He was told that they did, in fact that a whole offering of eggs had the night

The nomad gipsy tribes of India, of whom there are many, who live on rats and lizards and many curious things, throw up at times some compelling dancer, have the crudest and simplest and at times eccentric cults, and it is they who in certain parts have been given land by Government and confided to the efficient hands of the Salvation Army with interesting and notable results. No one other than Christians would be bothered with them, and the 'Army' and Franciscan Fathers were the best suited to tackle the *gamin* problem.

The Animists are those who will steadily become Christians, and some remarkable work has been done by the Church of Rome in this direction in the Sonthal hills, as well as by the other Churches. There is, as has been said, much room for really critical and scientific examination of genuine, elementary faiths, before they adopt the good or the bad of the great religions they may come into contact with. The majority of Animists in India proper, as apart from the Mongoloids, are among the Bhils, Gonds, Sonthals, Kolis, Todas and the like, of whom in some cases portions of the tribes in touch with civilization have been attached to the hem of Hinduism by being accepted as out-caste, but under the Umbrella, or have joined the freedom of Islam. It is a curious point to be noted that the out-castes whose touch is so destructive, are those under the Umbrella, and therefore included within the law as Sudras. Apparently if you are right outside, you are so negligible that your touch does not matter, which in itself is an allegory.

---

before been accepted. As there had been an unexpected increment of eggs on board his steamer, and he had seen his men making merry, he changed the subject, but on subsequent occasions he learnt that the Nats had been again and liked sandgrouse eggs on the Kurdistan road, and that the whole battalion felt that all was well. In fact Nats and ancestors are normally benevolent if properly revered.

Chapter VII

MODERN HINDUISM

THE HINDUS GENERALLY—BHAKTI AND THE MODERN SALVATION TEACHING—THE HINDUISM OF THE HUMBLE FOLK TO-DAY—THE ASCETIC MENDICANT—THE AUSTERITIES—THE VARIOUS SECTS OF MENDICANTS—HIS MAJESTY AT THE YOGI SERAI—HINDU CHILD MARRIAGE—THE ETHICS OF EARLY MARRIAGE.

The Hindus Generally

The origin of Brahminism and Hinduism, higher and popular, has been discussed, both in its first rise to great height and its reconstruction after the thousand years in the wilderness. As it grew after the reconstruction, so it stands for the most part to-day, except where severely in touch with modern Westernism. That aspect will be discussed later. Hinduism to-day is at any rate the census religion of over 160,000,000 people, of whom not more than seven per cent. are Brahmins. Of the remainder the number of the twice-born, in other words the high caste, is but a fraction, and the mass are the infinite variety of the low caste. The imminence of the ballot-box has however improved the status of the lowest castes in this way. When, as is likely to happen, parliamentary power may be given by communistic status, it is for the first time important that the number of Hindus nominal or otherwise shall be increased. The Hindu hierarchy is therefore somewhat less scornful of the pretensions of those outcastes who would come under the Hindu Umbrella.

In previous chapters several attempts have been made and with poor success to bring Hinduism to a definition, and that is still as hard to do. It is a strange fact, already suggested, that neither Brahminism nor Hinduism has ever founded a Church, as the West and Islam understand it, or instituted any central authority, and endeavoured to produce any creed, formulate a ritual or produce any recognised rule of righteousness. It is true that under this giant umbrella that the world—but it is curious to note not Hindus—call 'Hinduism', there have been countless teachers endeavouring to elicit a thousand different truths or rules of life from the Vedas and other religious teachings of antiquity! Follow any you like! none is greater or less than the other! has been the rule.

Hindus do not call themselves Hindus nor their religion Hinduism.

But here in the twentieth century when it is important that all who have anything to do with India, and in Great Britain every parliamentary voter is so charged, should know something of the subject, it is no undesirable thing that we should be able to describe by some short title the creed and rule of life of so many millions of our fellow subjects.

To get at all forward with the subject, we must fall back on some such account as a non-Hindu can indite of the matter. It would seem from all that has been outlined, that it may be summed up something as follows.

In theory Hinduism is the worship of an ineffable being in a Trinity or triple modification of the Godhead known as the Trimurti and sometimes as Brahm, with three, *persona*, Brahma the Creator, Vishnu the Preserver, Siva the Destroyer. This the theory by which the Brahmin or other Hindu theologist endeavours to explain Hinduism. Within this the Salvation cult can very properly pose

A Sivite Temple with Three Linga
Still in use in Southern India

as the highest thought on the same subject. In practice all the higher classes of Hindus worship, or fail to worship, in particular one of these three *persona*. So much is this the case that the worship of Siva and that of Vishnu are almost different faiths, and the term Hindu as applied to both has as much reference to ethnic origin, as it has to any similarity of religion.

Within these limits there are many manifestations of the God, and many forms from which worshippers select that which suits them, or that worshipped by the family from which they spring. When we come to the humble classes, partly Hindus or feebly associated therewith are the countless gods of the countryside, where each village has its own. To which it can be said that each and all are such portions of the divine influence as appertain to the dwelling-place or the avocation of the worshipper. A jockey who was a Vishnuvite might very well use the image of a horse as representing all that life meant to him, and therefore the representative of the Almighty Spirit from whom all good things flow. The barber might even exalt his shaving brush, and burn lamps thereto, and still be but worshipping in a dim way that Almighty whose dispensations have provided that he, the worshipper, should do his duty by God and man as a barber.

The foregoing is the theory, but so far as popular Hinduism goes it is far from the practice. Many people consider Brahminism as a distinct matter from Hinduism, and so in many ways it is. But if looked at from the point of view just described, it is but the difference from those who have thought out each point regarding the Almighty and all that appertains thereto, as let us say a highest order of clergy and theologists might do, and a public who, even those of pious mind, but watch and worship blindly.

To be a Hindu, or at any rate a nominal one, it is still but necessary to conform to the usual customs and ways of Hindus. There is still no religious law of life though there be plenty of customs, to which a man born a Hindu must conform. There is still no set of beliefs which a Hindu need hold. Belief is altogether free. It is true that the Hindu should consider the Vedas as inspired, the Brahmins divinely appointed as the priests of God, and that caste is ordained by heaven. Yet may a Hindu believe none of these things so long as he conforms.

The sacredness of the family comes first of all, so that nepotism is a duty.[1] The importance of the ceremonies is far greater than that of belief. The rules regarding food, occupation, marriage and residence are the things that matter. Break these and you cease to belong in the eyes of your neighbour and the community, to anything connected with Hinduism. The sacredness of the Brahman and the cow are as much an essential as ever.

And this again brings us to the question by another road—what is a Hindu? And the answer comes then—to be a Hindu a man must have been *born* in one of the social groups which since the beginning of time have been associated with Hinduism. To merely follow such ways and customs and worship as do Hindus, is of no account in entering the pale of real or twice-born Hinduism. It is said that Mr. Edwin Montagu, when in India, demanded in discussions with Brahmins at Benares how he could become a Hindu. He was told that his Eastern origin would help him not at all, but that if he fed a thousand Brahmins a day—and feeding Brahmins from time immemorial has been a very meritorious act—and then committed suicide, he *might* be reborn a Hindu,

[1]And this is one of the astounding difficulties of the public services in India.

and 'that was that', in the Aryan metaphor. His *karma* would dog him for ever. It may be realized from this how intensely apart and above the rest of humanity is he that is born a Hindu, meaning one of the twice-born classes. It will also thus be evident how astoundingly irreconcilable must be the points of view of Hindu and Muhammadan, of the Moslem, and to use their own phrase the *Musheriq*,[1] the Hindus claiming the only position that matters in this world or the next, the Moslem supremely contemptuous of the idolator or the man, as he understands it, of many gods.

It may also be here remarked that those who are *not* twice-born, but who from time immemorial have been in association with those who are, are infinitely more particular in the observance of ancient rule and custom, than those who are. That as a matter of fact will be recognizable as a very human trait. Thus will women too humble to be compelled to sit in *purdah*, often assume the veil, as their husbands rise in the possession of this world's goods. It once happened that the revered Sir Pertab Singh, the master of old-fashioned chivalry, a Rajput of Rajputs, was asked by an educated Indian who was travelling with him, how it was that he did certain things contrary to Hindu laws and customs. His Highness fell on him, "Why d . . . it!" he said, or words to that effect, "I am a Rajput, and what I do is good enough for me and for you." And from many points of view he was right. A Rajput of the 'Sun' or 'Moon' or, for the matter of that, even of the 'Fire' need fear no critic.

So much for the higher folk who may also devote themselves to the high service of any of the manifestations of the deity with all the energy of the '*Bhakti*', which has

[1] He who divides and shares his worship.

been already alluded to, that adoration and devotion which is to be found among the devout of all creeds, and which we may now explore. The Hindu who has steeped himself in Western ideas and Science, may hold the greatest contempt for the popular side of un-instructed Hinduism, and yet satisfy his soul with the higher side of *Bhakti*, and remain within the Hindu fold.

Bhakti and the Modern Salvation Teaching

While Christianity, as a religion to which people have flocked in great numbers, has made little progress in India among the Aryan races, nevertheless its effect on the national ethics has been remarkable. We need not refer to the basis of humane and modern laws and the suppression of some of the more cruel of the Hindu practices, but rather to its effect on the minds of the thinkers. The ardent supporter of Brahminism and of Buddhism, anxious to prove that he too proclaims a faith that has equal claims in moral and spiritual teaching, has been busy of modern times developing or furbishing up the more mystical of his faith's teachings. For centuries the contact with Christian ethics has gone on, and these have been studied with interest and curiosity by the learned of India and the Far East. The effect of this on Buddhism has been referred to already. In the recent years when the West and East have come into such close contact, the Hindu philosopher and theologist has been put to it to hold his own as the professor of great spiritual truths before the judgment of modern mankind. The teaching of *Bhakti*, so long cherished in the hearts of many Hindus, has now taken on a new meaning. It is openly talked of as a competitor with Christianity for the suffrages of the world. The earnest missionary of the day having long forsaken the attitude of contempt for the non-Christian religions, no longer talks heedlessly of idols, however much he may emphasize his reprehension of the evils which Eastern religions permit of unchecked and unchallenged. He realizes that there is great teaching, and has stirred himself to study it, so that he may the better know and explain where the non-Christian creeds join issue with Christ, and where they and Christianity can march together. In *Bhakti*, the adoration and salvation cults, have there had much study and their beauty and charm has been realized. It is not too much to say that these cults must have shown to Lord Irwin how far and how deeply the pious Indian and the Christian may share inspiration and experience.

To follow this form of Brahminical and Hindu belief, the whole gamut of popular Hinduism, its temples and its rituals, its braying of conches and clanging of gongs, may be thrown out, and the realm of thought entered, with no more selected surrounding that quiet and peace on a road untold.

The coming of the gospel of the Upanishads has been referred to and the idea that Brahm is joy, is life and death, and peace and comprehension, and how this great secret came to Brahmin minds several hundred years before the birth of Christ. Redemption, salvation, release are familiar Eastern conceptions before they were taught in Palestine, and the teaching that man must lose himself in identification with God is a very old urge.

Amid the coming of Greek and Tartar, of Mongol and Hun, the quiet and studious have sought solitude far from the madding crowd to make their study. Phalanxes and *gols*, *panch hazaris*, *hathi* and *howda*, Hastings and Harsha have passed them by, the hermit sat apart.

Here as I sit by the Jumna bank
  Watching the flow of the sacred stream,
Pass me the legions rank on rank,
  And the cannon roar and the bayonets gleam.

Is it a god or a king that comes?
  Both are evil and both are strong,
With women and worship and dancing and song
  Carry your gods and your kings along!

Fanciful shapes of a plastic earth,
  Both are evil and both are strong,
These are the fashions that weary the eye,
  These I may escape by a luckier birth,
Musing and fasting and hoping to die.

—LYALL.

But the *Bhakti* teaching held and holds more for the human than for the ascetic life, though the hermit spirit, and the search alone, are no doubt the failing of the Eastern Way. It may mean the complete identification of self in thought and deed, so far as humanly possible in the Almighty.

So much has the Salvation teaching caught the more sympathetic eye, that some missionary thought has even suggested that in a universal Christianity, the *Bagavad-gita* might even take the place of the Old Testament as a prelude to the Christian Gospels, and have even suggested that Bhakti-followers might possibly say the Lord's Prayer with Christians. To dispel this, while yielding to none his acknowledgement of the beauty and spirituality of the cults, Professor Rudolph Otto has recently written a treatise to compare the two.[1]

The atonement with the Deity of a soul craving the surrender of life and destiny and striving, the peace of

[1] *India's Religion of Grace and Christianity Compared and Contrasted.* —Translated from the German by Dr. F. H. Foster.

faith and trust, and the desire to be one with God, not for personal happiness but for Love of God, are granted as the aim and faith of the *Bhakti*. But *Isvara*, the Almighty as conceived by the Hindu mind, cannot be the Almighty as taught dimly by the Prophets of Israel and revealed by Christ. The conception of the two infinites are so different. Thus Professor Otto:

> "But the Kingdom of God in the Prophets and in the Gospel means something much more and much greater, than a mere demand for a decision by the individual in view of an eventual judgment. The coming Kingdom of God is first and chiefly that which the name indicates, the mysterious fulfilment and the goal which God has chosen, viz.: the last and final establishment of the '*malkut Jahweh*' over everything and all things and over the world itself. . . .
>
> "It has its roots in the soil of the old and specifically different prophecy of Israel of a day when 'righteousness' shall cover the land like water and when at last that for which the fathers hoped shall be real.
>
> "That includes a very different God from that of India. *Isvara* thrones in his eternity. Deep beneath him rushes the stream of the world, and humanity in *samsara*, in ever repeated circles of woeful birth and rebirth. In this world the wandering soul strolls, separated from *Isvara* by its fall, lost in the confusion of the world. Then He inclines to it in pure undeserved grace. Out of the infinite number of the lost, He raises His own to Himself . . . the world rushes on from one aeon to another, never dies, it becomes the abode of the honour and glory of God. It remains a *Lila*, a sport of the Deity, a concatenation without goal and end."

Thus the grace of *Isvara* is a thing apart, and we see that the 'Lord's Prayer' cannot be said under one umbrella by *Bhakti* and Christian, however beautiful and devout the *Bhakti* outlook.

Nevertheless we can see how ample is the space in which the two may work together for the good and happiness of mankind and for mutual understanding, trusting to the Almighty to choose the time of his harvesting.

The Hinduism of the Humble Folk To-day

But granted that there are many who through the ages have practised *Bhakti* and live to serve and obey, either their selected lord, or that supreme lord *Isvara*, as we have seen in the Salvation cult, what of the humbler and simpler folk, for those of high and low caste. What does Hinduism do for the humble and lowly? And here let us remind ourselves that high caste folk may be very low in the world's goods and the culture that should come from their possession. The answer is not by any means condemnatory. It is true that there is not much talk of adoration, of self-surrender, of *Bhakti*, but there is a great deal of homely good. Watching the contented and kindly masses of the people, one at once sees how much greater in mankind, given reasonable conditions is the 'original good' compared with the 'original sin.'

Hinduism, the worship of God in the form of Vishnu or Siva, their wives, companions, incarnations, or satellites, produces a general state of content and rough human duty, with a pathetic little uplifting of hands by the faithful hard-working wives, and the steady doing of the day's work for the wife and bairns by the menfolk. The sweet tinkle of the temple bells, the braying of the conches that summon to prayer, the conscientious and serious great uplifting of hands by the priesthood, all combine to make a life of reasonable stability and happiness. The popular festivals are eagerly and happily attended as in the mediæval ages in Europe. They are simple enough in their origins, the *Dussera* which is but the feast of Spring, the *Dewali*, the happy squib-popping *Dewali*, is but harvest home. The *Holi*, somewhat indecorous in its license, resembles that unbending of Greek and Roman days, when the prim and virtuous may let off steam by what is declared to be divine injunction, a truly human conception which *mi-carême* understands. But the tragedy remains that such good rule of everyday conduct that obtains, comes from the innate goodness of the people, rather than part of the rule of life of religion, that should show mankind a lead. It is not much of inspiration that men bring away from the temples, and yet they have much that is kindly and homelike in their call. And in all the little homes the good little Hindu wife says the family prayers for the tired lord, who sleeps and rests from his labours, and the bairns she stuffs with rice. In the south especially, among the Dravidian folk, the daily life is spoilt by the fear of devils and demons, and the bogy of ill omens. The temple are full of fearsome images, that perhaps are but inhibitions, and frighteners. Here among the humble ones and the outcastes it is that Christianity makes such strides, among the semi-castes for whom the priests and demons cater. Up in the Himalaya where the eaves of the cedar temples curl Tartar-wise and the great deodar groves cast cool shade, there we may find the hill folk enjoying some of the simplicity of the *Vanaprasthra*, the forest-hermits, and the little gongs and symbols bring a message of cheer to those of the valley who see the sun for perhaps two hours a day. Here indeed we see the village faith as we do in the northern villages, at its simplest and best. For when Adam delves and Eve spins the priest must be be the lifter-up of hands, and it is so the length and breadth of Hindustan. Both Vishnu and Siva, where the congregation see to it that their priests do not want, appear as kindly protecting divinities who will help a man through his troubles in this world. If a man wants more he can have it at the foot of the *guru* or *swami*, who will teach him the way of *Bhakti*.

Unfortunately no one will untie the knots of fear that make humble life so heavy. No one will tell the peasant that *bhoots* or ghosts do him no harm, that charms are not necessary and that even the dread *churel*, the ghost of the poor lass who has died in childbirth, and must haunt men-folk in consequence—you may know her because her poor little feet are turned backward—can do no harm to those who say their prayers and don't beat their wives.

Be it remembered that the simple folk and their ways and customs are the principal care of the British Magistracy, who alone love to understand them. The Hindu *intelligentzia* care little enough. Humble folk all the world round are the Briton's care, who study their needs, problems and future with often enthusiastic affection.

THE ASCETIC SECTS AND MENDICANTS

There are a little over five million Hindu ascetic mendicants who roam the length and breadth of India, having renounced all possessions, and who live work and care free on the generosity and holy instincts of the religiously minded. Who and what they are, and the good and the evil of a system which encourages such vast numbers from attempting any remunerative work in the community, is not very generally understood. The European in India classes them under a few general names, faqirs (which they are not, as faqir is strictly a Moslem religious mendicant), *gosains*, *sadhus*, *sannyasins*, *jogis*, *bairagis* and the like.

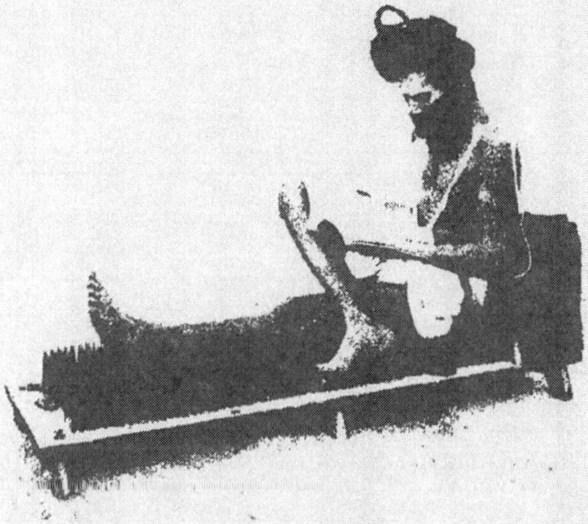

AUSTERITY. THE COUCH OF NAILS
Other things than Fame or Rank

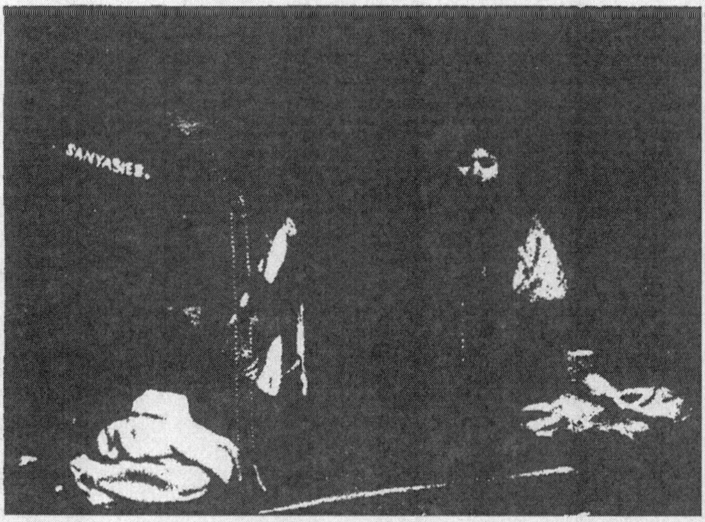

The religious ascetics are mendicants bound by vows of renunciation, viz. *gosains*, which mean lord, or master of passion. The ascetic orders were originally only open to the Brahmins, they were later extended to the twice-born, and are, with a few exceptions, now open to men of any caste. There are a few women ascetics, *sadhvin* (feminine of *sadhu*), but the publicity of the life makes it unsuitable for them, and the number are few. Now and again some widow, weary of her life of drab restraint, becomes a mendicant.

The term '*sadhu*', which means simply 'good', may be used as a convenient term for the whole class. All *sadhus* belong to one of the many religious orders entered under vows of renunciation of the world. All belong to and stay in various monasteries which have been erected by the pious through the ages. But monasteries are but their temporary habitat for their business is to roam the world, obtaining their subsistence from the charitable, and demonstrating to high and low before all worlds, that there is something else worth living for than worldly possessions and comfort. This object lesson they veritably perform, and do undoubtedly serve as a reminder of this cardinal fact.

The public receive them kindly and support them cheerfully. While many are earnest and genuine, some are impostors and time-servers. The public is perfectly well aware of those who are worthless, and those who are not, and while putting up with the faults and weaknesses are cognizant and appreciative of their good points. Naturally the people are apt to grumble and make jokes at the number of hungry mendicants who push their bowls before them, but pay up nevertheless, lest they be cursed or fail to earn the blessing of the gods.

Most *sadhus* wear a dress of saffron yellow, a few sects have other colours. All carry a begging bowl made of a gourd or coco-nut or sometimes of brass, and carry also a waterpot and a staff. A pair of fire tongs is often carried to keep evil spirits away, and convey a coal to the pipe bowl, and a pestle and mortar of *bhang*, their besetting weakness. Some go naked and are known as *Digambaras* or 'sky-clad', their bodies smeared with ashes which serve to keep off insects from their bodies and demons from their souls, as well as serve as an emblem of their humility. All wear rosaries of beads which serve to remind them of prayers and mantras. It is said that the rosaries of Christians were adopted from them.

Most of the ascetic sects are followers of Siva, a far less number follow Vishnu. The Saivites wear a rosary of 32 or 64 berries, the well-known knobly berry, of the *Rudrakshi* (*Eleocapu ganitri*) and the Vishnuvites of beads of the *tulasi*, the holy basil (*Ocymuni-sanctus*). Many *sadhus* wear also a necklace of human teeth, and a snake-skin round the neck. Their locks and face hair is usually unkempt and matted.

Most of the well-known teachers founded schools of mendicants who should go about and proclaim their teaching, and who are in fact begging friars welcome in households, and with many a Friar Tuck among them, dsepite their outwardly horrifying aspects.

The Austerities

The foundation of these orders is, as has been said, renunciation, *sannyasin*, and all idea of holiness in Hindu thought is based on *tapas*, which not only achieves holiness, but gives power over nature and over occult things.

Siva himself practised relentless austerities for countless years, and his followers but copy him. The word *tapas*, 'austerity', which really means 'hot', and hence the heat from pain, has an interesting inner meaning for in addition to that penance, and ascetisicm also means 'duty in that station of life, etc.' For the Brahmin, *tapas* means teaching, for the *Kshatrya*, or soldier class, protection of the community, for the *Vaisiya*, carrying out the allotted daily task of business or agriculture, and for the *Sudra*, service.

In addition to the act of renunciation and asceticism, which in many sects means the renunciation of all desire and passion, and involves celibacy, many tortures and rigours are involved. A well-known mortification is the couch of spikes on which the ascetic reclines. There is an authentic case of one *sadhu* who lay on one for over thirty years. Another well-known penance is to hold the arm over the head, till it is so stiff that it never can be lowered, and sometimes both arms are raised, which means that the *sadhu* can never feed himself. Nails uncut and curled like ram's horns is a popular culture. Swinging from steel hooks let into loops of flesh cut into the victim's back is also quite popular, and to be seen at festivals. All these severe penances and mortifications do not only bring intense feelings of satisfaction to the performer, and the sure and certain belief of the genuineness of his salvation, but do further emphasize what has been referred to, that there are other things in life that count besides ease.

The general control over nerves that results from fasts and the mortification do, no doubt, provide some inherent callousness to physical pain, and thus assist the seeker for righteousness in the weakness of his body.

It is interesting to know that the terrible spiked bed aforesaid, is derived from the circumstances of death of Bhisma, the leader of the great Aryan clan of the Kurus who was slain with so many arrows through his body that they protruded behind like the spikes of the bed of penance and remembrance.

The Various Sects and Mendicants

The sects of the *sadhus* are too numerous to describe in any detail but some of the more usual ones may be given. They are distinct from the mere recluse. An ascetic or recluse, is usually called a *swami*, which means 'lord' and is a term of courteous respect, and reverence, that entirely suits the gentle appearance and wholly benevolent life that the true *swami* leads . . . . the sort of person who is made to appear in the sketch in Chapter I. Mrs. Steel in her wonderful study of the Indian Mutiny, *On the Face of the Waters*, draws one outside Delhi while the stramash of the siege is on, with great faithfulness. Through the ages, men of presence and power and dominion have left the world in the East as in the West, to seek God and meditate on His ways. There is a quaint story of a European at some place of pilgrimage in the Himalaya, who had inadvertently let his impious shadow fall on the sacred aloof square of earth in which a recluse sat, eating his noontide meal. In disgust the Indian had risen and thrown down the hillside his food that was thus made untouchable, with an exclamation of horror. Then was he heard to say in English, "Tutt, Romesh Chander, Why should you, once a scholar of Balliol, be angry because that poor ignorant European has cast his shadow on you."

The great teachers of the past who have been briefly referred to in this short book, Sankar-acharya, Ramanuja, Ramananda, Kabir, all left sects behind them which remain, broken of course into sub-sects. But the majority of such are among the followers of Siva, and his fierce and bloody Goddess Kali, who can also be sublime and benign, as the sea rages and storms and subsides. The seven principal Saivite sects are as follows:

The *Dandins*, *Sannyassin*, *Bramacharin*, *Paramahamsa*, *Lingyat*, *Aghorin and Yogin*.

The *Dandins*, so called from always carrying a *dand* or staff, are solely Brahmins, and are also called '*Dasnamah*' or 'ten-names' from the ten principal disciples of Sankara. Their initiation includes a baptism, and the removal of the sacred thread of the twice-born.

The *Sghnyassins* include seven sub-sects, and are open to all castes. An initiate receives from the initiating *guru* his new name, the sacred *mantrum*, and is told the sub-sect to which he is posted.

The *Aghorins*, or *Aghora-panths*, are a strange sect, which is nearly dead, consisting of *sadhus* who have acquired a strange and repulsive appetite for the flesh of corpses, in fact, like their game high, and are reputed to steal corpses from burial grounds to satisfy it. Such a taste would be accepted as their peculiar method of mortifying nature and showing their humility.

Yogin, or *Jogis*, is the name for all ascetics who practise Yoga, who endeavour by restraint or disciplinc to obtain union of the soul with the Supreme. They are mystics and self-hypnotizers, and claim peculiar powers which undoubtedly some possess. Their founder was one Goraknnath, a follower of Mohendranath, of whom little is known. They are worshippers of Siva, disregard caste and normally live well.

The Vishnuvite followers among the ascetics are rather wandering monks than mendicants. Among these are the followers of Ramanukja, who are termed *bairagis*, who must be free from all world desire and passion and are pledged to celibacy. This and all the ascetic orders are really immersed in salvation of self, and there is little of the desire to lead others on the holy path, or anything of the order of Hospitallers about them. They crowd to the pilgrims and great religious fairs, but never think of doing a hand's turn to help the helpless, and the needy. That is left to the wandering Christian priest as shown in the scene in Chapter I, to the British magistrate and police officer with his *conshtabils*, who are father and mother to countless crowds.

Now and again some European missionary or other attempts to be *sadhu* and *sannyassin*, to live among them, learn their spirit and gain their confidence. But try he never so earnestly it is apparently beyond the powers of his psychology. On the other hand the Indian Christian to whom the mentality is inborn, does do so with success, gaining the affection and respect of those he meets. It is in this way that Christianity may come into its own.

The *Linga* cult of Siva naturally finds its way among the *sadhus* who follow that worship. Not only do many like the Lingavats carry a *linga* with them as sign and mascot, but they do so manipulate their poor person as by suture and what-not that their organs become afflicted with immense proportions, in the same way that some men's arms become fixed above them. In the popularity for *linga* imagery, such attributes add to their saintliness, and it is a matter of common gossip that women solicit their favours as a stimulant to their fertility.

His Majesty at the Yogi-Serai

At Benares there are of course many monasteries for *sadhus*, and there is one on the sacred banks of the Ganges where many congregate with wide steps that lead down to the water's edge. The *sadhus* there congregated would be of many sects and strange and horrifying as well as interesting appearance. While there, they are ruled by an old *sadhu* who, clad in leopard skin, and hung with rosaries and beggars' bowls, presides from a small shelter in the centre, a big kettledrum by his side, with which to call their attention.

It is related that His Majesty while in Benares was taken down to visit this serai, and bathing-*ghat* accompanied by a police officer, a surprise and incognito visit of great interest. Leaving their motor-boat at the steps, the King and his guide approached the old head-*sadhu* quietly. He like all his company were resting and drowsing in the noonday sun, the *jogis* and *sadhus* round the sides of the *serai*.

As they approached him, the old man sat up blinking, and staring at the new comers. "*Sahib*," he ejaculated to the police officer. "*Sahib!* You've brought the *Badshah*! That is not right without notice. Get up you *jogis*! Get up and salaam, you beggars! His Majesty the King!" and he beat great booms on his drum, so that ash-covered and leopard-skinned, deformed, loathely, benign and dignified, the holy men leapt to their feet. His Majesty had come to see the *sadhus*! Wah! Wah! and a very remarkable sight it was, as they danced and shook themselves and rang their bells, and then the King looked around and said a few words and perhaps disbursed something for creature comforts and the stomach's sake. As he came away, the steps of the bathing-*ghat* were crowded with such a weird and enthusiastic crowd as had not perhaps been seen since the days of Chandra Gupta.

Hindu Child Marriage

The problem of child marriage in India, is one which the public not only of Great Britian and the Empire but the whole civilized world has had prominently put before it, by the admirable writings of Miss Mayo. Miss Mayo's *Mother India* has been translated into most of the languages of the world, and no doubt her new '*Volume Two*' will be similarly honoured. I have used the phrase 'admirable' advisedly in this connection, because no book or sacred writings is likely to have done so much good to India. The complacency of the semi-Westernized, partially educated Indians, who have been pleased to lead such an entirely wrong-headed agitation against their great benefactor the British, was rudely shaken. They found themselves held up to the contumely of the whole world, and after accusing the British Government of hiring this American lady to abuse them for its own base purposes, have begun to try and set their house in order. They and those who suffer from the bitter inferiority complex which exists but in their own inner knowledge of themselves, are of no great account. What does matter for India and Indian womenhood, is that a certain number of educated Indians of real worth, who would come more into the open if they were guaranteed against intimidation, are really working to try and bring to their countrymen's ken the real gravamen of the indictment that Miss Mayo brought against them.

The circumstances of Miss Mayo's writing are worth recalling. She had come into fame in the United States, because struck by the campaign of abuse by certain factions in the States against their own administration of the Philippines, she went there to see, quite prepared to add her screed to the outcry. But to her surprise she found things very much the other way, that the Philippines was a centre in which depravity, evil terrible religions, and great savagery, mingled side by side with a better life. She found that the American services working in the Philippines were doing splendid self-sacrificing whole-hearted work for those lands and their unfortunate people. She therefore wrote to bless when like Balaam, she had come to curse. Then struck by the bitter campaign of spite that the United States to their shame, allows to go on against Great Britain in India, she thought she would come to see for herself here also, anxious enough perhaps to find that the evil repute was well deserved and to add her pen to its denunciators. She came, she saw, she travelled, she investigated. She was no Pagett M.P.; she stayed well over twelve months and then she wrote *Mother India*. The gravamen of what she said lies in the indictment, not necessarily of child marriage, but of the evils that may and do arise therefrom, and the callousness of Indian public to the abuses which were so frequent, and the terrible cruelties and horrors which she records. Further did she add her criticism to the general apathy of the Hindu mind, as regards all cruelties to the sufferings that follow maternity in closed zenanas, and to the general indifference to suffering of both human beings and animals. She traced the futility of the southern Indian races to their early marriages, to the excessive eroticism which Hindu imagery, however allegorical in intent, cannot fail to arouse. Never have a people been subjected to a lash so keen, nor a religion to so damaging a criticism. The false inferences that a reader might draw were that the indictments applied more universally that is really the case, and even in the hot-house of the south and west, were not so universal as *Mother India* seemed to imply.

The major portion of the indictment dealt with the evils of child marriage or the abuses that so often occurred, and they were trebly documented and established.

It is important to understand the ethics and the reason of the customs, buried as they are deep in the world's own knowledge of human nature.

The basis of *Mother India* is in reality the indictment of the power of Hinduism as a whole, to work for the good of human nature during its sojourn on earth. But the Hindu attitude is in reality the natural outcome of the doctrine of *karma*, if a man is but reaping as he has sown in a previous life by divine dispensation, who in this world should come to his assistance! But however that may be, before we join in the chorus of condemnation, let us probe a little deeper.

The Ethics of Early Marriage

In reading *Mother India* and its sequels we must not let our very natural horror and indignation get the better of us all together. Why does a religious and state system, from which comes *Bhakti*, and which has given birth to Buddhism tolerate now, and from the earliest times, this condition known as 'child marriage'. Nay, not tolerates but enjoins it. The answer lies primarily in the entirely laudable conception of the indivisibility and sacredness of the eternal partnership between man and woman, stimulated by that allegorical cult of *Yoni* and *Linga* just described. The new body for the wandering soul awaiting incarnation must be created, and no time must be lost, the young must mate, *les enfants poussent toujours*. Further the earlier the partnership the better, so that the characters may be formed together, and that each may fall into their allotted shares in the *samsara*, the rough and smooth of this mortal life. So much so good. Let us not confound another's bad practice with his good theory. That is a glasshouse in which no Christian dare stand. Still less as Harnack has said, 'confound one's own good theory with another's bad practice'.

Child marriage is also part of the ancient religious injunction to parents, which, though not practised by the migrant Aryans, seems to have followed soon on their arrival in the Indian plains, for it appears in the earliest law-books. "A girl should be given in marriage before puberty." *Dharmasutra, XVIII*, 21.

It is to be imagined that after the coming from the cooler uplands to the heat and the earlier physical development that ensues in warmer climes experience prompted some such change of custom. There is a saying "The tribe of Flynns know their own whisky skins." The Indian and the Arab also has always held the theory, held no doubt by the women as well as the men of the races, that his marriage before puberty was a measure prudently devised for avoiding the dangers which surround the period of adolescence in both sexes, and which can be so disastrous to the woman. It implied no sort of slur on Eastern character but recognized a biological fact known to most adult men, to many women, to some parents and a few teachers. It is the method of meeting it, and not the facts that may be in dispute. However that may be, because that was the ancient idea and the ingrained social custom, parents were and are extremely sensitive at having an unmarried daughter who has reached the age of puberty. But the problem of obtaining husbands, the expense of go-betweens and the difficulties of dowry, being ever present, there had arisen through the ages the almost universal practice of leaving girl children to die. This practice of female infanticide has successfully, but with difficulty, been suppressed by the British Government. A few kindly Indian minds have approved, and while most educated Hindus will render lip service to Western thought in this matter, in their heart of hearts they are probably indifferent. The East is so prolific that the death of an infant, before it has entwined itself round the parents hearts is no great thing. Besides there can be no fear of *karma* in the death of an infant girl to perhaps condemn her to a still harder existence on earth hereafter. So to this day when the police are not about, that basket of anxieties, the unwanted daughter, is encouraged to die.

Child marriages are of two different kinds and nature. There is the marriage of young children, who either return to their parents till the season of marriage is due, or in which the bride child is brought up in the husband's household under what is theoretically a watchful step-mother's eye, though the evidence given before the age of consent inquiry of India, showed how indifferent many parents were. The germ of the principle of such marriages is the same and rather more practicable in its application than that of the co-educationists. In due course this marriage will take the proper form of parentally approved consummation. Even under the best conditions, it will be from our point of view unduly early, and Miss Mayo attributes the poor physique and want of physical courage so noticeable in southern and western Hindus to this way of life. This point has been combated as scientifically debateable, on the ground that nature knows her own business best, and that the galloping or load-drawing horse is born of a very immature dam. But actual medical facts recorded in India cannot be refuted.

The other type of child marriage is that of an adult and usually elder man, with a child wife, often *en second noces*. It is in this class that Miss Mayo's innumerable horrors principally but by no means entirely occur. Here, however, let it be said that there are thousands of admirable elderly husbands of child wives. Small girls thus enter their husband's houses, sometimes in the care of an older wife, sometimes not, to be brought up, fostered, educated, cared for, with every sort of honour, kindliness and forethought, and there could be no question of premature wifely status. Such a proceeding is merely part of the indissolubility of the partnership rightly carried out. We see the same happening in the West when some elderly man may marry a ward, whose education has been his care for many years. Unfortunately the exceptions to the general right and worthy practice are far too numerous, and produce the horrors of which Miss Mayo writes, and in which as has been said, the gravamen lies in the apathy of public opinion, both to the injury to the victim and to the infamous perpetrator. Miss Mayo's new book, *Volume Two*, is designed to allow no gloss to hide the terrible facts. She exposes the attempts made to throw dust in the eyes of the United States, and especially in Mrs. Naindu's evidence and statements, which directly contradict all the facts acknowledged by Indians themselves. Miss Mayo quotes entirely from the Report of the Age of Consent Committee, 1928–9, which was the direct result of her first book, and the reports of debates on the subject in the Indian Legislative Assembly.

There the evidence of the ill-treatment of girls by young and old husbands is overwhelming as is also the almost universal representation that the custom, is good, enjoined by religion, and wrapped up in the affections and determinations of Hindu India.

In vain apparently do the few who know thunder against the evil. Miss Mayo traces the effect of the inquiry and the passing of the new Act. She outlines the previous efforts of the Government of India to introduce some faint control. In 1860 it was enacted that consummation before the age of ten years constituted rape. In 1891 a further bill raised the age of consent to twelve years, but there was and is little machinery for revealing any breach of a law, which is concerned with so intimate a subject. In the evidence before the Committee of Inquiry referred to, in which the evidence was fully published in the report, it is astounding to see how universal was the opinion, even by Indian medical men, that consummation before puberty even, was right and necessary. The opinion was expressed that Indian girls were eight times more sexual than men, and that they must be married before puberty or terrible trouble would supervene. A well-known Madrassi told the Court that it was essential that a woman must look upon one man old or young, handsome or ugly, as her lord and husband, and that the moment sexual impulse was aroused this would not be possible. Previous intercourse alone would save the position.

In the face of all this, which, if the situation is to be understood in full, Miss Mayo's *Volume Two* must be read, the Government of India stimulated and gave facilities for a Bill to be introduced by Indians themselves, placing it in the hands of advanced Westernized Indians and social reformers.

This Bill after the most astounding opposition passed as *The Child Marriage Restraint Act*, 1928. It was deprived in passage of most of its useful clauses, fines are leviable for an offence, and imprisonment may not be given for failure to pay. Miss Mayo dubs it the 'April Fools Act'. Further the British Government undoubtedly did itself a great injury in letting the Act be brought forward in the state of public opinion even as a private Bill. In the opinion of the public it *was* a Government Bill, and an unwarrantable interference with the Hindu religion and the private rights of man and woman. So much was this the case that during the months before the date April 1st, 1930, on which the Bill became law, hundreds of thousands of child marriages were hurried on all over the countryside.

Undoubtedly some of the unpopularity of the British Government of the present is due to the Bill's passing, though as Miss Mayo points out few are aware of its real conditions while prosecutions under its provisions have been almost a dead letter, and she quotes figures from the magistrates' courts to show that the average penalty for the rape of a child under its provisions is fifteen shillings! The offence, however, being marrying or giving in marriage too soon, the difficulty will be evident when we realize that when all is said and done, a husband and wife with their lives to lead are involved, and that the marriage cannot be annulled in the girl's interest.

The Bill, however much the dreary and pathetic horrors of the subject may have demanded it, does have the effect of manufacturing a semi-bogus class of criminal, and shows up very strongly the difficulty the British have always had in legislating, in opposition to the astounding evils possible under the Hindu religious system. It is also some witness to their courage in doing so in the case of Hindu female infanticide and also in suppressing the horror of Sati.

Miss Mayo quotes from the Bar Library of the High Court of Calcutta, the Brahminic law of marriage:

If a child is married before the sixth year of her life her parents go to a first-class heaven, i.e. attain the highest re-birth possible.

If between the sixth and ninth year the parents go to a second-class heaven.

If between the ninth and eleventh years only, to hell, viz. the worst re-birth possible.

It is also enacted that "He who takes a girl in marriage after puberty, is to be considered as the husband of a low caste girl."

These extracts show how the subject bristled with difficulties. Yet parents, mothers and fathers, educated people, told the Committee of Inquiry of the terrible results, including early death, that had attended their own child's marriages.

Evidence was further given that a girl whose *menses* commenced before she had married would consider herself out-caste and unchaste for ever. What a vicious circle! Poor British Government, and sad people! And at the bottom *karma*.

Interference in ethics is where the Anglo-Saxon is likely to slip up. Nevertheless it may be said on his behalf that he has succeeded in making the world his tribunal in matters Indian, and the tribunal demanded the attempt to rectify a scandal. World tribunals are in fact a nuisance, and our sympathies may lie with a Government which found itself impaled on the horns of a dilemma.

It is also interesting to note another point, this time an economic one. Marriages in India, as the great festival of eternity that leads to re-incarnation, are celebrated with great rejoicing. They are *very* costly, and custom in this matter is adamant. A man will marry and feast daughters of fourteen, twelve and ten at once, to combine three occasions and expenses in one. The new Act touches the purse of *paterfamilias*.

CHAPTER VIII

THE HIDDEN CULTS AND HARD SAYINGS

(A Chamber of Horror)

CULTS BEHIND THE VEIL—THE LINGA—SAKTISM—THE STRANGE STORY OF THUGGISM—BOMB-PARAST TO-DAY—THE BURNING WIDOW—TEMPLE PROSTITUTES.

CULTS BEHIND THE VEIL

IN the many religions of India, there are also many sects and brotherhoods developing some side of their creed, that can only be attained by selection and initiation, and which are provided with secret tenets, passwords and the like. In Hinduism their number is legion and the readiness with which they are entered, and the facility which they and the fraternities of wandering beggars, recluses and ascetics, can transmit rebellious and seditious movements, has been the source of much trouble to those in power through the ages. The peripatetic wanderings of countless *faqirs jogis*, *gosains bairagis* and the like, of the mendicant sects described, give occasional galore. Equally good, of course, are the opportunities thus given to those who watch what is in progress. With a country of countless millions of numerous races, different religions, broken dynasties, submerged peoples, the ferment below the surface of one kind and another is beyond belief.

How far some of these cults have imperilled the ordinary public is detailed in this chapter under the 'strange story of Thuggism,' that 'death that walked by day as well as by night,' and whose suppression alone is one of the brightest jewels in the necklet of stars that will sparkle for ever on the British neck. The story of *Bomb-parast*, bomb-worship, as it goes on to-day to the same adoration or patronage of the horrible Kali, as animated the Thugs, may give some folk to think. There is a well known story of the Mahratha prince to whom Kali the wife of Siva, in the devastating vein of the Sakti, the vampire, the were-wolf and the praying mantis combined, appeared. Beside his bed she stood, her eyes flashing fire, as in a Soviet chamber of justice, *Main Bookhi hun! Main bookhi hun!* (I famish! I famish!). Whereon he arose and slew all his brothers, that the blood craving of the Goddess, might be satisfied—the Goddess to feed whom Mrs. Curtis lies in the Lahore Cemetery, and many a magistrate and police officer working for the people has been bombed and shot of late to make a Congress holiday.

But while secrecy make go with savagery, it also goes with cults as harmless and beneficial as British Freemasonry. The Hindu sects have all a ceremony of initiation a password and what is more prized a 'Word of Power' that magic word which, if uttered by the man who has so subdued his nature as to be near paradise, may move mountains and achieve empires. The 'Word of Power' in all the inner cults of the great religions is the one thing sought for, that Word that boomed out from the idol in the great inner temples of Egypt, the 'Word of Power' that was on Aaron's rod, the word of which the Psalmist says 'When the sea saw that it fled,' the Word that was on Solomon's ring, and which Jesus, said the Jews, having found illegitimately, used to work his miracles. The 'Word of Power' that all men seek 'The *gyatri*' that must never be said, the sacred cry of

A GIANT PHALLOS

The Polished Linga in the Kaillassa Cave at Ellora

obscure meaning '*Om Mane padmi hum!*' 'The jewel is in the Lotus.' The Shiahs themselves follow largely an inner and secret mystical cult both the Twelvers and the Seveners, and the Agha Khan's bathwater it is said assisting in the latter. Mysticism is too secret to be taught on the highways and at the temple doors. The Sufi too are eminently a secret benevolent philosophy and across the great water the *Phi Beta Kappa*, attempt the same.

But the cults of India too that are secret, are often gross, and fringe on the great worship of the *Linga* of Siva as the representative of life and death. How this cult of Siva or Mahadeo works in allegory as well as in lust, and from allegory how it leads to the obscenities of left-handed Saktism, must now be described.

THE LINGA

We now come to that aspect of Hinduism and also of the more refined and spiritual Brahminism that is such a marvel to the outside world. It has been explained already that for Siva, the Destroyer, who has also by analogy become to be regarded as the creative side of the Almighty, is represented in all Sivite temples, in the village shrine, and under the roadside tree, by the male organ of generation, in a state of erection. It is made of many materials and of many shapes and sizes, temporary and permanent, of mud and of rice, of grey limestone and polished black basalt many feet high, of copper and bronze with agate tips, a few inches high or of great size. The Hindu sect called the Lingayats, both men and women, carry one as a precious personal mascot on their person, generally in some silver or bronze case. Some are made of conventional type, some the *mukhi linga* have faces carved round the sides, some are extremely life-like, lines and veins being represented and figure in allegorical interpretation. It is the custom in more cultured and sanctified circles to explain this phallic worship as pure allegory. Here is an allusion to Brahmin the lord of all from the *Bhavagata Purana*:

"Bara Brahman, the Lord of Sakti and Siva, the womb and the seed of the Universe, who like a spider, forms it in sport, through the agency of Sakti or Siva." Sakti being the wife of Siva.

It has already been explained that Sakti is the female side of the deity to whom is given the anthropomorphic wife. In sheer allegory and simplicity it might be represented as the womanly and kindly side of all great issues. In the practice of humanity the idea is inseparable from grosser views. In the carving and drawings of myriads of Hindu sculptors and artists rein is given to the most fantastic and often gross presentments of the ramifications possible in such conceptions.

In the *Kuvalavanandi*, the well-known religious work of Appayya Dikshiti, it is written:

"Sakti is the form of the pleasure derived from *guthya* (the female organ). Siva is the *Linga*. From the union of these two, it is the cause of all joy in the universe." Which is a profoundly wise saying no doubt, and worthy to be believed. The allegorical interpretation can be, of course, appreciated. In this sense Kingsley's kindly apologia for the mental conceptions of an ecstatic nun may be remembered.

There is a very popular brass representation that can often be seen, of the *Linga* of Siva with Parbatti, his wife, embracing it in a state of ecstasy.

The Gudimallam *linga* of which a drawing is given therein, is alluded to as essentially realistic in *Elements of Indian*

Icongraphy, written by Gopi Matra Rao, the Director of Archæology in Travancore, is an example of the more realistic style of presentment. It is also to be noted that the *Linga*, whether life-like or conventional, is always represented as standing in the *Pitha* representing the *Yoni*, the two inseparable emblems of the world.

Sir Ramkhrishna Gopal Bandakar, who writes on the religious systems of India, definitely says that it is the actual generative male organ of Siva that is contemplated and worshipped, but that ascetic contemplation deprives the idea of all grossness. To which it is perhaps not unfair to say, that such teaching while showing the way of light may also be holding a candle to the devil.

He also adds "Ramaniya tell us that the Kapatikas maintain that a man who knows the essence of the 'six marks' attains the highest bliss by concentrating his mind on the soul seated in a female organ." Hear also from the *Bhagavanta Purana* of Siva,

"He whose seed is raised up, whose organ is raised, who sleeps aloft, who abides in the sky, the Lord of Seed, who produces the Seed".[1]

Eastern writers, who in some sense compose apologia, give equally forcible examples of the worship of Priapus in mediæval times. That is so of course and within the knowledge of all students, but while one might be the cult of a few eccentrics the cult and outspoken allegory of the *Linga* is for all folk and all ages of a vast people, so different in this matter is the outlook of East and West. In an Hindu household, the first sign of approaching juvenile virility would be as great a matter for family rejoicing as the cutting of a wisdom tooth in the West, while the writer has known a boy of thirteen, the eldest son of a cultured family, a boy-scout by the way, who rarely

[1] So far as imagery is concerned, c.f. 'His horn shall be exalted

abandoned his scout dress, demand his right to be present at the accouchement of his elder sister, a demand recognized as just and according to the custom, and acceded to.

One of the difficulties of European tutorship bringing up young Indians of quality, is to prevent the very early entry into sexuality which their mothers and female relatives are anxious to encourage, and many strange stories of the bombarding of lads with naked women in dark passages could be told. Again the only comment is how different the conception of the greatest mystery of the world is that of Hindu and civilized Westerner. In Europe the old fertility cults have long ago died away, but is interesting to note that those who have studied the 'witchcraft' cases in comparatively recent years, know that it was an organized survival in Celtic countries of an old cult, arranged in covens of the magic thirteen, and that the devil who always appeared in a black dress and horns was but the master addict of the cult in his robes not unusually some worthy of the district.

Saktism

We now come to the really secret cult of *Saktism*, which existed more in Bengal and to some extent in the South of India, and prevails with varying intensity in modern times. It has been explained that *Sakti* is the wife of Siva, and the word in its general sense applies to the worship in anthropomorphic guise, of the female side or influence of the special attributes of the Godhead that the god in question represents. Siva is often represented as part man and part woman. There is a carving representing this to be seen at the Indian Museum at South Kensington. The left half has a female breast and the right half a pronounced phallus, and it represents the idea of joint responsibility for fertility and creation. The beholders may attach to it as much allegorical or material comprehension of this mystery as they are capable of.

But, indeed, we must again realize that the East sees no shame in that mystic communion that keeps the world alive. If the volition of a man and a maid may summon a soul from the infinite where is the shame? Both in the Qoran and in the Darma Sutras folk are instructed to 'call upon the Lord' on their most intimate occasions. It is the unlawful occasion, and the unholy connection that deserve obloquy:

The Saktas are the worshippers then of *Sakti*, the wife of Siva, the female essence, power and force in life. They have the complex that is sometimes to be met in the writings of the somewhat dotty super-feminist, that the female is the superior and dominating force in the world and must be allowed to control it. You sometimes hear such folk inculcate the teaching of this truth to small boys from their early years.

In Sivaism generally the *Yoni* or *Pithi* or *Guthya*, the female organ of generation is an object of adoration allegorical or otherwise. In Saktism, this is specially developed. A favourite ornament in brass or stone is a *yoni* surrounded by nine lesser *yonis*, with ornamental margins and borderings, known as the *Sri-kakra*. Male followers of *Sakti* are urged to contemplate the might and force of woman, and by contemplation to even believe themselves as women. Some are able to induce the feeling of the catamenia, a state which curiously is also observed by those German students of 'inversion' and other phenomena connected with *psychologia sexualis*. But in accordance with the figure of Siva just described, *Saktas* are divided into two sects, right and left handed.

The former while astoundingly suggestive in their worship and ritual, are at least decorous, worshipping the *Linga* and the *Yoni* as figuratively as possible, adoring however the statues and paintings of the nude woman in their daily devotions and the *Sri-kakra*. The left-handed Saktas are far otherwise. Their lodges and meetings are held in secret and secluded places, the object of their devotion is a living beautiful woman set before them and the cult of *yoni-parast*, or *yoni*-reverence, the worship of her organ of generation, is a very realistic one. Their seances at which both sexes attend, are accompanied by excessive, religious ecstasy which develops into extreme license under the effect of stimulants. Also no one in Hinduism asks many questions as to the doings of those who conform to the Hindu customs as described. Any Sivite who became so inclined can become a *Sakta*, and it is nobody else's business, so that who are, or are not, followers and their numbers, would not be easy to ascertain. In fact the meetings of the left-handed sect are probably as secret as those of the old Cumberland witch covens, and many Brahmins are known to be Saktas.

In view of the extraordinary way in which the imagery of fecundity is introduced into the Hindu worship in many ways, it is not difficult to understand the custom which permits of the existence of the *Devadasis* [1] the dedicated temple prostitutes, against which westernized Hindus do nowadays protest. Nor is it difficult to understand the evil side of child marriage of which Miss Mayo writes so strongly, but which is so bound up with the life of the people. The temple prostitute custom the writer has known adopted by the incumbent of a Moslem shrine, appalled at the decay of its popularity, endeavouring to take a leaf out of the Hindu book, by providing such attractions. It

[1] Vide the last section of this chapter.

is to the credit of Islam, that even if a temporary increase of congregation did result, that the prestige of the shrine fell to zero in the district.

To make an absurd but realistic comparison it is as if Dean Inge added a troop of geishas to the choir of St. Paul's to attract worshippers. Perhaps it would have that effect in so ribald a world.

The imagery of fecundity is to be noticed in almost every Hindu picture and sculpture, some times openly realistic, usually only noticeable to the initiated which would, of course, include the whole Hindu public. A favourite symbol of the male and female is the inverted triangle, that standing on its base, being the male and that on its apex the female. Superimposed the two are emblematic, not unsuitably, of eternity. This emblem is also known as the Seal of David, and as such is often to be seen over the doors of Jewish lodging-houses in our English sea-side towns.

The beautiful corridors of the Indian Museum at South Kensington, are full of the most wonderful specimens of all that is great in Indian art. The religious carvings and paintings in their beauty, delicacy and fervour as also at times, in their fecund suggestiveness, are well worth study. I notice that in one specimen of a temple frieze, where all the male worshippers have what the mediæval writers have called the 'Lance couched' the latter has been cut off by a Victorian curator with a chisel, in the interest of his visitors which seems hardly necessary.

It has been explained that some of the great Madras Gopirams as temples are terribly indecent, such indecencies being explained as having the same intention as the mediæval gargoyle on Christian churches. They make it as impossible for a European to take a European woman round the temples as it is to share the sight of the Pompeian cupboard statues with your companion.[1] And this it is that makes Lyall write of

> "The organs of birth and the circlet of bones,
> and the loose loves carved on the temple stones."

It is not too much to say that in the lesser Hinduism there is no sexual vagary or bestiality, even to the maintenance of a harem of animals that would not be explicable as an injunction from the deity to honour him and the universality of Nature in that peculiar way, so much is the vagary of the eccentric accepted.

Another instant of the sanctity and popularity attached to the conception of the *yoni*, as an everyday mascot and luckpenny, is the name of a cleft in the rock on Malabar hill in Bombay not unlike that to be seen at Freshwater, in the Isle of Wight. It is known as the *Yoni*, and to pass through it is a pious act. In fact not long ago a very famous Hindu potentate made a special trip to Bombay for this purpose of carrying out this very rite, in connection with his desire for an heir. Childless Indian women will make innumerable offerings and prayers to the basalt Linga of the Sivite temples, without any sense of indelicacy. In this connection it is to be remembered that the possession of a son is an absolutely necessity for the proper leaving of this world, and of ceremonies that shall insure an elevated and not a degraded re-incarnation. Indeed it may perhaps be said that the doctrine of re-incarnation itself does imply a special emphasis on the Fecundity Cult in religion, for every birth allows a waiting soul to tread one more stage on the way to salvation.

[1] The Black Rock Temple in Chittagong is notorious. No lady visitors record their names at the visitors' rest-house.

The Strange Story of Thuggism

Among the many strange things that the British, the impure, accursed British of the Ghandi saga, have done to or for India is the destruction, the rooting out lock, stock, and barrel of the sacred cult of Bhowani the Goddess, as expounded by her followers, the Thugs, or *Phansigars*, the stranglers. The story is so astounding that it should never be forgotten. From the time of Akbar at least, but possibly for thousands of years, there had existed in India, unknown, but strangely suspected of the people, a widespread secret fraternity whose cult was the murder of the wealthy for the sake of their goods. For generations merchants, travellers, and others had disappeared, without their relatives having the least knowledge of what had become of them. They and their families perhaps would just pass out of existence. Now and again some prince or ruler might exterminate a gang on whom he had lighted, but merely an *ad hoc* extermination for crimes brought home. That he had touched on a widespread organisation of crime tinged with fanaticism, was never known if ever suspected. Only in a country such a prey to rapine, war, and disorder, as was this continent of India before the *Pax Britannica*, could such a thing have been possible.

Many years passed before the British came to suspect it, but about the period 1810 suspicion began to be aroused. The word *Thug* had for long been a word of ill omen for lawless theft and robbery, concerning which no very clear ideas existed. In that year the Commander-in-Chief in Bengal issued orders warning sepoys moving on furlough in small parties to beware of Thugs.

Some facts had already been collected, and as early as 1816, Dr. Sherwood wrote a paper in the *Literary*

Journal of Madras, which purported to reveal the whole story. This paper was later proved to be admirably correct, in its description of the dread organization and its methods, and it seems rather more than incredible that the British had not put their hands to the problem earlier. On the other hand, they were busy with the settlements after the wars of 1803–5, and the disastrous effects of the Cabinet's and the Court of Directors' reversal of many of Lord Wellesley's policies, and the aftermath thereof, in the Mahratta and Pindari wars of 1817–19. The disorders in Central India due to the destruction of all responsible government after the Mogul collapse, and the rise of those nests of land pirates, termed Pindaris, in the jungles of the Narbudda valley, gave a great impulse to the cult of Thuggee.

Law and order there was none, all merchandise and bullion moved by pack animals, and this threw many merchants into the hands of fellow travellers who might or might not be reliable. The Thugs had a golden opportunity, and in the numbers and characters of innumerable masterless men had a great field for recruitment.

What exactly, then, was this cult? It was a vast secret society which both Moslems and Hindus joined, based perhaps on some hatred of the wealthy and fortunate as persons whose prosperity should rightly be given to others, and immediately devoted to the conception of Kali, another name for the female side of the great Siva, Siva being, as explained, the Hindu *persona* of the deity in regard to life and death, birth and burial—that part of the Godhead whom men must fear and please in the daily duties and joys of life. Kali is specially concerned with everything cruel and hard, as well as much that was good and pleasant. Under her form of Bhowani, the Thugs rendered her homage, swearing their allegiance to her both as directress and protectress. Their cult was, in effect, the obtaining of wealth for their own personal use, and in the heart of every initiate there soon arose a sacred joy in depriving people of their lives for the mere sensual gratification thereof—a form, in fact, of Sadism, and of that unholy joy with which Soviet female executioners have put their prisoners to death.

It is presumed that at first the statements put forward by Doctor Sherwood, were considered too hideous and monstrous for belief, but several members of the Indian magistracy had begun to study the story very closely. By 1830 active operations against Thugs as ordinary thieves and murderers began, notably in Bundlekand and in Western Malwa, part of the districts in which the Pindari oppression had been so severe; but as yet no attempt to recognize the system, and attack it as such, had been devised. Three well-known magistrates in Central India, Major Borthwick and Captains Wardlow and Henley, had tried and executed many Thugs for the murder of travellers, but without any public attention being drawn to the crimes as part of a cult and system. At this time the number of murders were so many, and the audacity of the Thugs so great, that the Government was forced into probing the matter to its roots. Several distinguished civil officers turned their attention to Thuggism. It was not, however, till the confessions of one, Feringhea, were received and analysed that an inkling of all that the cult stood for was gained. For some little time, as a mere matter of police practice, certain of those sentenced were offered pardon if they would peach on their confederates, but only in the hope of clearing up their special gangs.

The disclosures of Feringhea were so appalling and

so incredible that at first the famous Colonel Sleeman, or Captain Sleeman as he then was, would not believe them. But as the confession said that thirteen of the victims were actually interred in the very grove in which Sleeman was camping, this led to exhumations, which only too truly bore out the Thug's revelations.

From this time dates the serious and organized campaign, and the formation of a special bureau which developed into the Thuggee and Dacoity Department—dacoity being that organized robbery under arms which is still the curse of many districts, and into which India is only too prone to relapse.

It was found that Thuggism was rampant all over India, from the Himalaya to the edge of Ceylon, and east and west from Cutch on the Indian Ocean to Assam on the Burma border. There were few places in which the confessions of the informers were not verified by the exhumation of their victims. Special officers for the suppression of the cult were now appointed in various parts of India, among them being Captain Sleeman and Meadows Taylor, as well as others equally famous in their day.

From Feringhea and other informers the whole machinery was laid bare, and it is from Feringhea's confessions that Meadows Taylor wrote with little expansion the celebrated *Confessions of a Thug*, the recent issue of which in "The World's Classics" series, with a note by Mr. B. A. Stewart on the whole business, is well worth perusal by all interested in crime of a strange and inhuman kind, and of how the great police officers of the day dealt with it. They may also meditate on the ease with which such cults may arise again were at any time events in India to follow the course of those in China. Dacoity,[1]

[1] Robbery under arms, often accompanied by crude terrorist atrocities and tortures.

THE MAJESTY OF ANCIENT HINDU TEMPLES
The Indra Galepa in the Caves of Ellora Deccan

Thuggee's not too distant cousin, is as we have said always endemic in the countryside, as the annual police report on any one of the provinces of India will reveal.

The origin of the cult is lost in history and wrapt in mystery, and Colonel Sleeman thought that it might owe its origin to the early wanderings of Tartar and Mogul tribes, then pagan, in the provinces of India. The Hindus claimed the divine origin and meddling of Bhowani with the affairs of men, and certain it is that Thugs, whether Moslem or Hindu, observed Hindu ceremonies which undoubtedly pointed to a Hindu origin. It has been likened to the cult of murder and robbery known to exist in Persia in Sassanian times, and to that Old Man of the Mountains, the head of the Assasseens —a cult of which, as explained, in its (harmless) modern form the Agha Khan is head—in any case it is a mystery not likely now to be unravelled.

According to their legend, the Thugs were a body consecrated by Bhowani or Kali to her service, sworn to protect each other, and observe certain rules and ceremonies, and to spend their time in removing human beings of wealth from the world, their wealth passing to the Thugs to be shared on a basis of equality and brotherly love. New members were sworn in by terrible oaths and penalties, and were to be thrice faithful one to another. They were bound by their oaths to shed no blood but strangle their victims, and to be sure that all trace of their action was removed. Strangulation was carried out by a sacred silk handkerchief, in the use of which all Thugs were made adept. The initiated worked in gangs, with a perfected drill, and always consulted omens before any enterprise, which they abandoned if the omens were unpropitious. Before they started to carry out a murder, the *nishan* or burial pickaxe, which was the emblem of the Thug was specially consecrated and called *Khussee.* Meadows Taylor gives the invocation to Bhowani (Kali) before the gang started on their enterprise.

"Mother of the Universe! protectress and patroness of our order, if this expedition be pleasing to thee, vouchsafe us thy help, and give us an omen of thine approbation."

Then were the omens sought, the *Philao* on the right to be answered by the *Thiboa* on the left. The gang or its leaders would start as ordinary travellers, get into touch with travellers, render them services for days, be hired as escort and the like. They would be told off for their various duties . . . the *Bhutearis* who looked for a suitable spot for the murder and burial, the *Lughais* who dug the graves, buried the victims, and obliterated the signs, the *Bhutotes* who did the actual strangling, with the *roomal* or handkerchief. Always was some sign arranged. The Thugs and victims would be at meal together, the *Bhutote* alongside his victims. The sign would be some such remark as, "Bring tobacco" or "Bring *pan*", and in a moment the victim would be on his face, the *roomal* round his neck, and the Thug making the twist of his wrist and thumb which finished the deed. Absolutely without mercy were the miscreants, women, children, servants, young and old, beautiful or the reverse, with a Thug to each, whole parties would be dead on the signal and buried within half an hour in the *bhil*, as the selected burial grounds were called.

After each accomplished murder, the gang would offer thanks and consume a consecrated communion supper in honour of Bhowani. After the manner of the East, headmen of villages, state officials of towns and states, would be in the gang's pay, without perhaps, unless they were themselves retired Thugs, suspecting more than that they were local bandits who paid handsomely. Here and there some especially clever and courageous official would even blackmail them, and probably suffer for his pains.

Once the British Government realized what they were up against, and had placed officers of energy and experience on the track of the system, matters began to move. In the official report the working of the Department for repression between 1831 and 1837, resulted in 1,772 being dealt with, 412 being hanged as murderers and 1,059 being transported for life, a further 483 had been accepted as approvers and 120 more were under sentence and 936 awaiting trial. A special colony of approvers under protection was formed at Jubbulpur, where their descendants are to this day, and where any tendency to lapse could be watched. At the same time the Bureau was searching for 1,800 more whose names and crimes were known. The number of *bhils* or burial places that were opened and found full of bodies, often close to the most frequented halting places and even within cantonments, was astonishing, and it was estimated that many thousands had perished annually for many years at the hands of this impious and growing cult.

The years of anarchy referred to had given opportunities beyond the dreams of prayer, and many recruits as had been alleged in the first reports. For many years the Department of Thuggee existed and kept watch on this movement, lest it should show its head again, and also on various secret and subversive movements, subversive of both civilization and the British Raj. Eventually it was merged in the Criminal Intelligence Department, whose annals will make the most astounding reading in the world, in which crime mingles with Siva and Vishnu in a manner unknown elsewhere. The stories of the modern Bengal secret murder cult and the Babbar Akali movement, of which Sir Michael O'Dwyer has given some account, are all tinged with the same fervour that animated the darkest side of Thuggism. And it is just this presence of some ancient horror existing beneath the outer surface of perfectly reasonable political aspirations, which has been a source of trouble to many a kind Viceroy desiring only India's good.

Bomb-Parast To-day

A '*but-parast*' is a worshipper of idols, a '*sag-parast*' a worshipper of dogs, and a '*bomb-parast*' is one who has put a bomb in the shrine of Siva or Kali, that he may worship it and gloat with hungry Kali on the blood that may flow when he shall throw it. The murder trials that have followed on the sedition and secret murder cult in Bengal, and indeed throughout India, show in their records how the Hindu student depraved and often injured by too early eroticism, turns to the suggestiveness of the murder-monger, and worships the nitro-glycerine bomb as the apotheosis of his goddess. The bomb flung at Lord Hardinge, as he rode through the streets of Delhi killing his aide-de-camp, and plastering his own back with gramophone needles, was hatched in the nitch of some domestic hearth where the kindly Vishnu should have presided. The haunted young Sikh, who rushed a few months ago into the little English household at Lahore Cantonment, to kill with a sword the young mistress, and chase and injure her terrified children in the garden, amid the roses and the lupins, was but a victim of the *bomb-parast* that has been allowed by the hot-air merchant to penetrate peaceful life. The Indian police officer, himself a villager, at his duties, Sir John Simon and his kindlyCommission, Mr. Saunders, the best of police officers, the magistrate giving prizes to Indian school boys, are last year's crop of the uplifting of hands before a bomb in a nitch, in the *piscina* of some household, before which the little lamps flicker, and the lad is fed with the cult of the implacable. As Bhowani and Kali were the patron saints of Thuggism before which ruthless blood cult, young nor old, maiden nor matron, man nor boy were spared, so does the *sakti* of Siva shed her blessing, in the opinion of her votaries to those to whom Kali makes her cry '*Main bookhi hun! Main bookhi hun!*' (Intone it nasally) "I want blood! blood! blood!". At Cawnpore she got it brimming over, the women's breasts sliced off, the children, Hindu and Moslem, torn asunder to make a Hindu Holiday, by many hundreds. '*Main bookhi hun! Main bookhi hun!*' So easily does this hysterical East with its perverted world cults changes from simple kindly humans, to demons.

The student and the assistant editor of the rag, that but exists to inflame students and pays its way by advertising the most potent aphrodisiacs[1] among them, are the nidus of the bomb-cult, and the show-room of the sour super-minds who conceive it.

Even the most kindly may fall to this blood-lust, the saintly *Baba* Ghandi may at any time be afflicted like his followers at Cawnpore with this desire to destroy. Mother Kali, the Goddess involved by Thugs, the Queen of Small-pox, and the *sakti* of all that is evil as well no doubt, as explained of much that can be good in this incomprehensible medley, presides in many a nitch that was built for softer and kindlier influences. *Kali ma ki jai!* (Victory to Mother Kali!)

[1] The majority of the Indian Press, even the most reputable, find the aphrodisiac advertisement their principal source of income, as reference to their advertisement columns will show.

Burning Widows

It is not perhaps unfitting that widow burning shall be dealt with in this chamber of horror.

There are four matters in which Hinduism has received the execration and contempt of the civilized world. They are worthy of understanding, and of study as to their origin and extent of the evil. They are or have been as follows, and three are part of the religious system. They are the burning of widows on the funeral pyre of the husband, the cruel treatment of widows who do not burn, the making away with female children and the universal custom of child marriage. *Sati*, the burning of widows on the funeral pyre, was stopped by the British in the days of Lord William Bentinck, in the last years of the reign of our William IV. That wise and benevolent Governor-General obtained the general consent of the more enlightened Hindus of Bengal, before legislating, but the legislation was only enforced with difficulty, as it ran counter to the wishes of the people and indeed of the women themselves.

The custom which dates from the period of Hindu reconstruction at least is an injunction in the *Vishusmriti*, or Traditions of Vishnu, and runs thus:

> "If a woman's husband dies let her lead a life of chastity or else mount his pyre."

The presumption is that the life of chastity was so difficult that the pyre was preferable.

But the whole story is mixed up with the wholy admirable sentiment and theory, that the union of man and woman is life-long and the one permanent thing in the world. It is the same principle that underlies the matter of child marriage. It is the habit of the ribald to say that the custom of the widow mounting the pyre, was the only protection an Indian husband had against poisoning at his wife's hand. But the real aspect is that if a man dies his wife it is believed, and she believes it too, that she has brought him bad luck. So she often went to the pyre joyfully, all the more so, that custom deprives her of all her ornaments, compels her to shave her head, to always wear a whitelike shroud, and to become a drudge in her mother-in-law's house. In practice, many, to avoid this fate, flee and join the congregation of prostitutes, for except under certain modern conditions to be explained, none will marry so accursed and unfortunate a wretch. Little child widows whose marriage has not been consumated must follow the same rule. Though *Sati*, which incidentally but means 'good woman', has been abolished by statute for close on a hundred years, nevertheless hardly a year passes without the attempt of some widow to be '*Sati*.'

Sati was practised much later outside 'British' India, and in 1839 a large number of wives and concubines were burnt at Lahore on the occasion of the death of the old Maharajah Ranjhit Singh. The country round would be wildly excited, and women would come from many miles round to touch the hem of the *Sati's* garments and to receive the widow's blessing. Tremendously elated and in a state of ecstatic hypnotism the woman would seat herself on the pyre, with her husband's head on her lap, amid vast crowds, and many priests blowing horns. The unfortunate would then be held down on the pyre with long poles so that there should be no weakening of resolution, while the shrill horns and conches drowned the cries of the victim, brought perhaps to her senses by the lapping flames.

It was a cruel remorseless act, and sight, only intelligible if we think of that re-incarnation in a higher state to which so meritorious a *karma* would ensure. It is only the Goddess Kali, the hungry Kali of '*Main bookhi hun*' fame, who could approve so terrible a happening. But a very few years ago a case of *Sati* occurred on the Ganges, and the police only got information late. They arrived on the scene to find a badly burnt terrified widow, who had escaped from the pyre and was lying in the water. Had they not arrived she would no doubt have been drowned by the Brahmins.

The famous Job Charnock, who founded Calcutta, rescued an unwilling widow from the flames and married her.

The hearts of the people and the opinion of the women is still probably subconsciously in favour of the rite of *Sati*, and it was not till 1860 that the Government of India was able to introduce a law making the re-marriage of widows in India legal.

All over the countryside will be noticed by the curious, close as a rule to big tanks and river banks, little slabs of stone, with the soles of a pair of little feet cut thereon in relief. They denote the place where some brave and loving Hindu widow has burned with her husband, he but a corpse, she alive and in the heyday perhaps of her youth. *Main bookhi hun! Main bookhi hun!* cries the Goddess Kali, 'I hunger for blood and sacrifice'.

Temple Prostitutes

We now come to that most astounding of ancillaries to popular Hinduism, the existence of the *Devadasis*, the *Muralis* or Temple Prostitutes already alluded to, that shares the shade of the same umbrella as *Bhakti*. It is not till we go back to the *Hierodouloi* of ancient Greek life that we find any parallel. But it is to be remarked that a religion which tolerates the imagery just described, can but regard *Hierodouloi*, as the proper corollary of the worship of *Linga* and *Yoni*. If the *Linga* of Siva in the flesh is to be dreamed of and imagined, what more natural that on the principle of education as adopted by Mr. Whackford Squeers, an interview with a Devadasi should follow adoration at the foot of a garlanded *Linga*.

Devadasis are women dedicated to the service of the temple from infanthood, who, in addition to the duties of a deaconess or a 'tidyer', are at the service of the worshippers and also of the priests. Nor, as has been said, should there be matter for surprise, since the corollary is but the outcome of the teaching. In a community where the exposure of an infant daughter is so often practised, the sale or dedicating of such to temple service presents no difficulty. It is perfectly true that the reformers, members of the Arya Samaj and the like, and those who write to the English magazines, do very strongly on the westernized side of their characters condemn this ancient habit, however much an involuntary inner self may condone it. They have been severely taken to task for their pains, as endeavouring to destroy the only honourable self-supporting career open to Indian women! to which one can but again exclaim at the many points of view in this Eastern kaleidoscope.

The Devadasis are as a matter of fact, usually married to an idol or a tree and have their marriage lines. They often retire after a not uncommendable life according to Hindu lights, and live in a village within the odour of sanctity and respectability. It is, of course, to be understood that such women are not the appanage of every Hindu temple, not perhaps very many, but of enough to be notorious. One of the most notorious and ancient of the temples with Devadasis attached, is Jejuri not far from Poona, where the women were known as *Murlis* or *Muralis*, and were 'married' to the God Khandoba.

There being no central Hindu religious authority as explained, there is no one to lead an effective campaign against this institution. When we study the many points in which Hinduism cries for reform, notably the attitude of the educated Indian towards child marriage, as evidenced before the 'Age of Consent Committee of Enquiry', and the general tone of so much of the teaching and practice that shelters under the Hindu umbrella, the Devadasi scandal appears in its true proportion as by no means the greatest. Nor is it easy matter for legislation, apart from the objection to interfering with custom in advance of popular demand, for it brings in its train the whole question of prostitution which no country in the world can solve. In this particular question as might be expected, the problem in India is different altogether from other countries. In the first place to a great extent Indian women are better provided for so far as 'sheltered life' is concerned, than those of the West. The normal courtezan's trade is plied by three classes, by the children of courtezans born, and brought up to the profession perhaps for generations, by the *gamin* women of the outcaste tribes, to whom no one in India will admit a soul to matter, and who take to the life as a duck takes to water, and thirdly by Hindu widows, who the dreary joyless slavery prescribed for by custom, drives to escape and become denizen of the '*chakla*', Were Hindu customs as regards widowhood widely reformed, this source of supply would fail.

Connected with the subject is also that of the highly trained dancing girl, and her rôle and position in the world,

and the fact that as in Indian life there is no social intercourse as we know it in the West, and no meeting ground where cultivated man may be entertained by women, the courtezans latticed alcoves are the rendezvous of the man who would hear music and the gossip of the day, and are often frequented for that purpose only.

Chapter IX

THE RELIGIONS OF INDIA IN THE TWENTIETH CENTURY.

THE BRITISH GOVERNMENT AND RELIGIONS—HINDUISM UNDER STRESS—THE BRAHMO SAMAJ—THE ARYA SAMAJ—THEOSOPHY—ISLAM IN INDIA TO-DAY—MODERN BUDDHISM—LAMAISTIC BUDDHISM—CHRISTIANITY TO-DAY.

The British Government and Religions

It is not out of place here to glance at the attitude of the British Government towards all religions in India, and in this connection it is well to realize that Great Britain, whether the East India Company or the Crown, have never been under any misconception as to their position and duty in India. They have realized that they had attained to their magnificent position as the successors to the Great Mogul and the throne of Baber, by a most astounding chain of circumstances of which the goodwill of the mass of the Indian peoples, added, of course, to the unassailable prestige of British arms and enterprise whenever the exercise of such was necessary was the principle factor. The British having shown themselves capable of, in Buddhist metaphor, 'taking up the burden', and having the courage and patience to piece together the broken fragments of the Mogul Empire, India rejoiced tha* it should be done.

In doing so the religious sentiment of the country, the antiquity of Hinduism, the sanctity of the Brahmins, the purity and dignity of Islam were recognized. If India was to be managed and built, any interference with religions was out of the question. The policy was unhesitatingly adopted and continued, of allowing religious activities full swing according to immemorial custom, and all confirming all religious endowments and properties as soon as substantiated. It was only when anything connected with law and order, with the clash of different faiths, or with customs that outraged beyond bearing some world sense of civilization and humanity, did the Company's Government or the Crown think of restraint.

So much has this been the case that the Company was accused by early missionary effort of being astoundingly callous of the rights of Christianity, and the duty of missionary enterprise. We are now wiser, and know that the Company realized how eager would our enemies be to accuse us of designs against religion. How easily these are set about and with what malice pursued by subversionists, the history of the Indian Mutiny was to show. Thrice wise was the precaution that forbade British servants to take active part in proselytism. Missionary enterprise must prosper of its own merit and according to its appeal to the people only, however unsympathetic to the eager missionary spirit such a policy might seem.

It is not too much to say that the great success, the unimaginable and unbelievable success, that has been met with in the picking up of the thousand Mogul pieces, is due to the wisdom of a policy so entirely removed from that which attended the institution of Portuguese dominion. The difficulty which besets all such positions, and other countries than Great Britain holding similar position have the same trouble, is that religious activities sometimes approach so near to politics of a seditious nature, as to come within the limit of taboo. That has in the past been more noticeable with Islam, where sovereignty is almost an essential for logical existence, but in such entirely admirable and permissible movements as the Arya Samaj, there has of late been a politically submersive bias developed in one of the wings, that no self-respecting government could tolerate. In the blend of dominion with sympathetic development, and self government within limits, these possibilities have aspects which will at times, tax both character and statesmanship to the uttermost.

Hinduism Under Stress

The essential point now to ask ourselves is what the Hinduism of to-day has to offer India, whither it is trending, and what it can offer to its own people first as a religion, and secondly as a race-maker and promoter of workaday contentment and happiness. It has been shown that it is to-day essentially what it was from the beginning, still a thousand different divisions philosophically admitted under one umbrella, and by the philosopher esteemed to be the many inventions surrounding one god and one allegiance. Having no head, no central authority, no ritual, and no decalogue, it presents a million difficulties to the reformer or the modernizer. As through the ages, great leaders have appeared in modern times endeavouring to reform, endeavouring to make both a religious entity and a civilized rule of life. The difficulties of all such is still the solid mass of the Brahmin opinion acting almost unconsciously with mass inertia, but as hostile to its own reformers as to any missionary religion from outside.[1] The want of a central authority, able to instruct and to lead, is now glaringly apparent.

How uncompromising this mass resistance is, will be more readily understandable if we read the evidence on the 'All India Committee on the Age of Consent,' conveniently epitomized for the average reader in Miss Mayo's *Number Two* already discussed. The solid wall there presented by two classes of witnesses, nay by three, the educated orthodox Hindu, the eager reforming Hindu, and the educated women, is astounding. All were agreed that progress was impossible, that the great edifice of uncontrolled unshakeable custom and religious essentials, in the structure of ancient and modern system, was against all reform. That is what Mahavira the Jinna, Ramanuja, Shankar-acharya, Ramananda, Kabir, Baba Nanak, and in modern times the founders of the Brahmo and Arya Samajs,—as great men as their predecessors,—have been up against.

On the other hand it is true that we, both modern British sympathizer, and modern Indian reformer, living at the modern rate do emphatically expect time to do more for us than it has ever done before and can possibly be expected to do. We want to see the edifice grow, under our eyes, we would lash the slow hauling lines of sweating slaves who are laboriously bringing a pyramidical block into its place, forgetful that a Buddhism took five hundred years to rise, let alone to wane, in India, and that two centuries did not make much of Christianity as a world force. But round this great immalleable mass of Hinduism, which is fairly soluble at the edges, the eddying of many waves has some effect, each twenty-four hours that the earth moves round the sun, and

[1] And at heart bitterly hostile to a rule which has made the Brahmin citizen amenable to civil law, and put him to death for murder.

will slowly have more, if we will let the generations have the time they need.

We who are outside Hinduism would wish to see the various movements for good grow faster, to see the tenets of the Arya Samaj grow firmer, to watch the effects of re-action to Christian ethics that have been so noticeable, having greater results. We would see character grow faster among the people, and see southern and western physique, which owes its inferiority to the age old customs discussed, yield some quicker improvement. In fact we want to see chalk having a more lasting effect on granite than seems possible in nature.

During the nineteenth century two great movements have arisen almost entirely, in their particular lines, due to the re-action from the pressure of Christianity, and to a lesser extent that of a peaceful and therefore a more spiritual Islam. They are the Brahmo Samaj, more noticeable for its lofty aims and the greatness of the intellect of its members, than its numbers, and its younger imitator the Arya Samaj, which by the very nature of its intentions, and aims has drawn a far greater following. They must be outlined if we would see the future of Hinduism—*Samaj* but means 'Society'.

THE BRAHMO SAMAJ

The Brahmo Samaj or 'Society of God Almighty' came into existence in 1828, at about the time when Lord William Bentinck's lead as Governor-General, in wider humaner matters was being felt. Added to this the accumulated influence of some remarkable Christian missionaries, among whom such names as Kiernander, the Baptist Marshman and Dr. Duff, as well as the young Chaplain Henry Martin, will long stand out.

The founder of the Samaj was a very able and earnest Bengali, Ram Mohan Roy, who like Ramanuja, in the centuries before him, and many another, was struck with the moral and religious degradation of his countrymen. He realized that reform was necessary, but also realized that it passed human wit to disentangle from Brahmin teaching and Hindu thought, any basic divine principle on which to found a movement of reform. One of his own following, a Brahmo, has thus described the condition of Hindu Bengal at the commencement of the nineteenth century.

"The whole country of Bengal was steeped in the most debasing form of idolatry. The moral and spiritual aspects of religion and its elevating influence on character, had long been lost sight of, and in their place the grossest superstitions had taken hold of their national mind. Men were clinging to dead form . . . encouraged by the priestly class, whose power depended on their continuance . . . fostered by . . . Brahmin preachers who made their living . . . by working on the imagination and credulity of the multitude. Thus . . . the most extravagant mythological stories . . . were implicitly believed in by the masses. As a result revolting practices like *Sati*, the throwing of children into the Ganges by their mothers, the suicide of devotees beneath the wheels of the car of Juganath became fashionable, and were looked upon as great acts of virtue . . . a comparatively new form of idolatrous worship called Tantrism[1] . . . which encouraged open indulgence in drinking and sensuality, and many other secret and demoralizing practices, introduced during the last six or seven hundred years."

Ram Mohan Roy saw clearly that reform must come from a new or at any rate clearly enunciated religious

[1] *See* Chapter VIII, "Saktism."

people. From the first he set his face against idolatry, and the Samaj has stuck to this point for over a century. He believed that he could found reform on a basis of a monotheistic doctrine, which as explained has always lurked behind more serious Indian thought. It is believed that it was the study of Islam that first forced this thought on him, reinforced by his subsequent study of Christianity. In this connection he published translations in English and Bengali, of the Upanishads, declaring that they inculcated the pure Theism he was in search of. He also published extracts from the Gospels which he called 'The Precepts of Jesus'. He opened in 1828 a place of worship, and composed with the help of his friends a form of ritual.

At this time he was a man of fifty-six, and died in England five years later where he was buried as a Unitarian. It was he who in 1829 helped Lord Bentinck suppress *Sati*, in the face of strong orthodox opposition, but after his death his Samaj fell away until a new force appeared on the scene in the shape of another reforming mind. Devendra Nath Tagore came of a prominent Bengal family whose father had been a close associate of Ram Mohan Roy. With twenty-one new members a solemn covenant was drawn up, in which the faith of the members in a Supreme Being was enunciated, and in which each undertook to lead a new life, something like the undertaking at Christian Baptism. Devendra Nath Tagore led the Samaj for many years, surviving till 1905, and being known as *Maha-rishi*, the 'Great Seer'. He looked on the society as an orthodox form of Hinduism and not a revolt from it, but his followers thought otherwise, and so early as 1865 were greatly steeped in Christian teachings and the fervour of religious reform. The leader of this party, Keshab Chander Singh, who had joined the Samaj in 1857, became an enthusiastic student and admirer of the life of Christ, and on this point split with Tagore, and formed the larger party. Coming to England he was made much of in both 'Church' and 'Chapel', but seems to have grown too uncompromising to carry all with him, even demanding that he should be treated as an inspired prophet, and another split occurred. Brahmoism then went through many vicissitudes, sometimes as a mere theistical body, sometimes as a reforming body, protesting against the evils of child marriage, and much upset when Keshab married his daughter to the Maharajah of Kuch Behar before her fourteenth year.

The Samaj continued without gaining the wide adherence hoped for it, keeping outside any final movement towards Christianity yet always admiring and sympathetic thereto, and it still remains a reforming force in Bengal. The late Lord Sinha was among its members and, as has been said, it is in the calibre rather than the numbers of its followers that its importance lies, and it has undoubtedly stood as a force in the moral uplift of the Hindu community in Bengal. Where it may trend it is impossible to say, and the force of Hinduism has turned more generally to the Arya Samaj which must now be described.

The Arya Samaj

The story of the Brahmo Samaj brings us to a modern Hindu movement of quite a different type, with great possibilities for good and with, in some respects, a sinister trend referred to, in that it cannot avoid a political aspect. The Arya movement has an origin in something of the same spirit as the Brahmo Samaj, but with a different inclination. It is the very definite outcome of the modern movement in eastern countries that draws its inspiration from two different springs of power and action. *Firstly*, the spiritual stir which the coming not only of Christian teaching into the East, with far more force than in the day of stray and wandering Jesuits or of the Nestorian stream. *Secondly*, the fact that wherever the West has had authority, Christian outlook towards the treatment of man and beast has been incorporated in the law. On the top of this comes science and university curricula, which challenging even the less intelligent of Christian inventions and legend, has put eastern religions in the dock of reason, In current slang which expressively describes the situation, Hinduism, Islam and Buddhism have had to 'pull up their socks', if they were to retain a shadow of self-respect, and be able to face the world's intelligentzia and humanitarians. What has been termed a renaissance has been in progress, and the Arya Samaj is one of its Hindu children and the biggest thereof.

Arya Samaj means 'Aryan Society,' and implies only the Aryan of India, whom the world, but not the Aryan, calls Hindu. In this connection may we pause again to marvel, at what has already been referred to, that Hinduism is not a word that the Hindus know, though we have a parallel perhaps in the use of Nestorian, which is a word that ancient Church neither know nor recognize.

The Samaj had its origin in another of the line of teachers and reformers, Swami Dayananda Sarasvati, whose original name was Mula Shankar, a Guzerati Brahmin of a wealthy family. Seated one night as a lad before the image of Shiva in an all-night ceremony he noticed that mice ran over the idol. Demanding of his father how such indignities could be, he received the unconvincing reply that as in this evil age the deity would not come to earth, the faithful worshipped representations of stone. So early as 1846 he ran away from his home to avoid the usual early marriage, and in search of *maksha*, that state of beatitude of which the early teachers spoke. Wandering with religious mendicants for fifteen years, visiting many shrines, he attached himself to a well-known Sadhu, and studied and practised Yoga. A mendicant, by name Brahmandand, taught him the orthodox Vedanta philosophy, of the *atman*, the identity of the human soul or *atman*, with the world *atman*. He then became a *sannyasi*, a world-renouncer, and led the ultra-ascetic life that such an association involves, his saffron robe, his blanket, and his beads his sole possession. Then it was that he took the name of Dayananda Sarasvati. He abandoned Yoga on discovering that it was based on a false conception of the human anatomy, and also the orthodox Hindu philosophy, and came to believe in a personal God and the reality of the world, the very opposite of the theory of *Maya*. The working of this spirit and the evolution of the doctrine of this Swami are of special interest, as they have been seen by living man, and show us how his prototypes who came to the same conclusions must have developed, Ramanuja, Ramananda, Kabir and the like. As he grew older he came under the influence of a blind Brahmin of Mutra, that holy town on the Jumna, where lie the countless ruins of the Hindu temples destroyed by the fury of Mahmud of Ghuzni, which is still as holy a Hindu locality. This recluse the Swami (lord) Virjanada Sarasvati, became his last *guru* or spiritual director, and under him Dayananda studied deeply in the Sanskrit writings. Here yet was little of the West and no outward signs of any Christian teachings or controversy. It was the old introspective Aryan mind searching deeply to find that countless others had 'been there before'. The Swami Virjananda actually lived at Hurdwar, the famous holy place of Hindu pilgrimage on the Ganges, where the endowments of the pious provided monasteries and *ashrams*. At the feet of the blind Swami the now aging Dayananda was learning the need for reformation. Like the teachers of the Christian Reformation the cry was 'Christ Crucified' and 'Back to the Gospels'. To Virjananda he pledged himself to fight against Puranic Hinduism, and to try and bring back the old simple Hindu teaching and spirit before it was cumbered with the thousand inventions of Dravidian devil India. He was soon hated by the orthodox Hindu teachers, yet despite opposition, the people in this land searching always for light flocked to him, always wishful to escape from . . .

> "The myriad idols around me, and the legion of muttering priests,
> The revels and rites unholy, the dark unspeakable feasts.

From his guru, Dayananda learnt what he was to preach 'Back to the Vedas' which was to be the clarion of the Arya movement.

Christianity came under his notice but more to enable him to steal its thunder, to see where his teaching could meet it on equal terms, and how he could adequately re-act to a faith, that was obviously a challenge to the best that his Vedas could offer to mankind in travail and in quest.

So far back as 1863 Dayananda was on the move, and was one of the 'Sons of Thunder' preaching openly and loudly at Hurdwar and elsewhere against idolatry, challenging pundits to discussion, denouncing the toil of pilgrimages, attacking idolatry, yet always supremely orthodox on his basis. As the Christian Reformers taught '*Back to the Gospels*' and the Wahabi leader '*Back to the Qoran'*, so Dayananda Sarasvati taught '*Back to the Vedas'* so that for long no Brahmin, of whom he was one, dare openly call 'Crucify him'.

For a while he insisted in talking in the Sanskrit as a Christian priest might have insisted on the Latin, rather than the understandable Romance, and only later taught in the vulgar tongue. So outspoken and so popular did he at last become, that his brother Brahmins made several attempts on his life while men of humbler castes adored him. At Benares in the heart of orthodox Brahminism and traditional idolatry, amid the countless temples and the extravagant carvings, he called on Hindus to scrap the six philosophies and to root out the Puranas, whence came all mythology. In Calcutta he met Keshab Chander Sen, the leader of the Brahmo Samaj, something as St. Augustin met St. Columba on the Wear, and it is to be regretted that he did not imbibe some of Keshab's reverence for Christianity.

In 1874 Dayananda, by now widely famous, produced his work on Hindu Reform, '*Satyarth Prakash*' or 'Exposition of the Truth', which while laying down the tenets of the Arya Samaj, that is to say of all who were prepared to follow, quite unnecessarily set forth also to attack Christianity, Islam, Jainism, and Sikhism, and in that respect showed how conscious his Hinduism was of its failure before the world's opinion.

It was not till the next year that he actually founded the Arya Samaj at Bombay. He formed it on the model of the Brahmo and its child the Paratha Samaj, but would not amalgamate. The Arya Samaj now went forward with great enthusiasm, being well received in all directions, countenanced by the Hindu princes and by the educated progressive mind throughout India. Then indeed Dayananda struck for trouble. He founded his *Gao Rakshini*, or 'Cow Protection Society'. Nothing very much has been said about the veneration of Hindus for the cow in this book as it is indeed but a manifestation—but it may here be remarked, that apparently fortuitously, the originally economic injunction to preserve the cow for its useful services to mankind, has grown to a fanatically religious feature in Hinduism, with many attendant evils, which Miss Mayo did not fail to notice.

Since the cow includes the bull and the bullock the ramifications are extreme. The Hindu farmer must not destroy his useless and lame cattle. So as no one dare grow beef ostensibly for the market the Hindus sell their barren cows and lame draught cattle to Moslem graziers and no questions asked. The latter then fatten them for the beef market. This accounts for the great inferiority and trivial cost of beef, a penny a pound being an ordinary contract price. The Moslems are the eaters of beef and have exalted in doing so where they are in the ascendancy, in the face of the shuddering Hindu. Among the seventy million potential Moslem beef-eaters there are a few hundred thousand Europeans, and beef even at a penny a pound is an essential article in the British soldier's diet. Wherever the British authority extends great care is taken to see that Moslem and Christian beef is slaughtered where it can give no offence. But when racial and religious animosities are running high, it is a common thing for Moslems to subscribe to kill a cow and throw the carcase into a temple, while Hindus may retaliate by throwing the impure pig's flesh into a mosque. The form of insult it will be noticed, while equally severe is intrinsically different, one being sacrilege, and the other sheer insult, with little to choose between them. At times the British magistracy are much concerned in preventing such displays of liberty and fraternity.

The formation of the *Gao Rakshini* did very definitely make for strife and ill-will, but curiously enough in his first edition of the *Satyarth Prakash*, Dayananda did permit of beef-eating and it has been suggested that his second society was an endeavour to wipe out the enmity that his earlier liberalism must have evoked. The Guru died in 1883, at the age of fifty-nine, but not before many thousands had followed his lead, and not before he has left sufficient driving force behind him to give a better hope for Hindu folk in a modern world, than any other indication.

Summing up the doctrine it may be said that Dayananda, a follower, taught the unity and personality of God. He advocated spiritual worship and condemned idolatry. It has even been rumoured at one time in Hindu circles that he was a secret British agent for breaking down Hinduism!

He deemed God and the individual soul as having no connection. He taught re-incarnation and *karma*, with some simplification. He dwelt on the importance of this life, declared that the Vedas foresaw all modern invention, and declared that all the names of deities in the Vedas were but alternatives of the Almighty.

His definition of the human soul is as follows: "The immortal eternal principle which is endowed with thought and judgment, with desire and hate, which is susceptible of pleasure and pain, whose capacity for knowledge is limited . . . even that is the soul."

Caste he rejected, and as has been related he always vehemently denied that he was outside ancient Hindu orthodoxy.

One troublous hard saying he has left behind, in countenancing *Niyoga*, "a temporary union of a person with another of the opposite sex for the raising of issue, when marriage has failed to fulfil its legitimate purpose". It is presumably that he wished to come to the rescue of women avoidably barren, but there is room for countless difficulties.

The Samaj, unlike Hinduism, has understood the principles of organization and control, with eleven Indian and provincial assemblies, and local congregational control of each local Samaj. Its possibilities as a great force are therefore considerable, and it has at times much troubled British authority. While not in itself a political body,[1] it does include many of the modern intelligentzia and the university youth, among whom the present hysteria has ran riot. Its dangers for the peace and prosperity of its members outrun its proper mission is considerable. It also poses as the leader and prophet of Aryan nationality, whatever that may mean, and not only fairly enough tries to counter fresh Moslem propaganda, but has set itself to bring back to some sort of a Hindu fold those who have left it during the centuries, an activity which of course calls forth counter activity on the Moslem side. It throws some sort of rope to the lesser untouchability, and has been misguided enough to be intensely hostile to Christianity. If it recognizes the latter driving force, as likely to remove the wretched step-children of the Hinduism untouchables, from its hard household, that would be a reasonable Aryan outlook for fear, but it has preferred at any rate, in many quarters hostility and hatred, an attitude which has not helped it. Perhaps its chief danger as a religious force is the apathy of the young university student to all religion, and this may drive it to accentuate the political bias which up till the last few years has been a not unnatural concomitant of some of its activities. On

[1] But, in present conditions, growing more so.

the other hand it suffers from the ingrained fissiparous tendencies of the country.

In 1892 the Samaj, like most such movements, underwent a split, two parties emerging the "College Party" which was against all restriction, and urged freedom from Hindu rules of diet, while the *Mahatma* Party considers the Arya Movement as strictly Hindu and enjoin prolonged Vedic study, and prescribe a vegetarian diet. The total number of Aryas in 1922 was close on half a million.

Theosophy

It is not possible to glance at the Brahmo and Arya Samja, without a hasty glimpse at that other movement of half a century ago, which arose when the great stir was arising in Hindu minds fifty years ago, as the result of Western and scientific study, viz., Theosophy. The Theosophical Society was founded in New York so far back as 1875 by Colonel Olcott and Madame Blavatski, and moved to India in 1878. It had three aims:

i. The formation of a real brotherhood amongst men of all nations and religions.
ii. The study of Aryan and especially of Oriental religions.
iii. The investigation of the occult powers in man.

Madame Blavatski claimed to have intercourse with supernatural beings called Mahatmas. Much conjuring and trickery took place at Madras which was exposed, and Madame Blavatski fled from India and she and her rose-leaf manifestations did not return.

The Society however, continued to flourish in India under Colonel Olcott, and after him under Mrs. Annie

Besant. Every religion to Theosophists is legitimate and right, and proselytism is to be condemned. Nevertheless Transmigration and *Karma* are maintained among their own. The influence of Theosophy in India is no doubt due to the countenance it gives to the ethics of Indian idolatry, and many a Hindu, it is said, has been restored to content with its own beliefs because of the support of Theosophy. The society has certainly done much for education in India, but has always been extremely hostile to Christianity. Spiritualism and clairvoyance and the the progress from 'plane' to 'plane' of power and knowledge has always been connected and intertwined with the tenets and practice of the society, which still numbers many adherents in India with branches elsewhere. Like the Aryas, it embraces many of the classes to whom destructive politics are a modern amusement, but who are largely classes whose hand has never kept their head, whose power in history has only been on the *escalier*, and who are unfortunately supremely ignorant of the real patient agricultural often Dravidian India, for which they would legislate. Its potentiality for good has not been exercised to the full. It is perhaps Britain's tragedy that with all the wealth of kindly assistance, and with all the prospects offered, the intelligence of the members of these societies is not offered freely to the work of building. Theosophy however, is one of the intellectual currents that go to make up awakening Arya.

Islam in India To-day

It is not too much to say that India in a great measure is the principal home of real Islamic thought and orthodoxy, in view of the laxity of observance that has long characterized Mesopotamia, and the collapse of Turkey and Russian

Moslem Art tainted with Hindu Floridness
The Tomb of Tippu Sultan at Sringapatam

Turkestan. It is idle to deny that the world change after the Great War has entirely altered the proud position of Islam throughout the Middle East. Islam inherently provides one law civil and religious, and without dominion is an anomaly. But so long as there was a Caliph of the East so long had orthodox Islam a spiritual Home on Earth. There has, as in Rome, long been something of schism between East and West, with a Caliph of the West in Morocco and of the East in Constantinople, but the former is but a local influence.

It is even true the Caliphate of the East was none too serious in modern times. Abdul Hamid as a Caliph in being, had for political reasons of his own endeavoured to rouse an enthusiasm in himself which the Moslem world did not feel, and his Caliphate has never had the position that Turkey hoped for. Nevertheless it was Constantinople, the great capital of the East, that was still the nominal head of that Faith that deliberately aimed both in matters temporal and spiritual in emulating the Roman Empire. When young Turkey repudiated all religion as a thing that a state could possibly be interested in, and expelled both Sultan and Caliph, with the dual personality went the ecclesiastical head, the Sheikh-ul-Islam. So long as there was a head even largely nominal, so long was there some one to whom Islam could pin allegiance, and such co-ordination as was necessary to keep religious entity. The assumption by King Hussayn of Mecca, of the Caliphate, 'cut no ice', though he was infinitely better entitled than any Sultan of Rum. But the disastrous collapse of the great Moslem people in Russian Turkestan, and of holy Samarkand was almost as severe a blow as the disappearance of Constantinople. It may be remembered how certain Moslems of India in the years after the war, looking for a stick to beat the British Government raised a great to-do over the terms of peace that were proposed to Turkey. This movement termed the *Kilāphat* or Caliphate movement, did from misunderstanding attract to it many a sincere Moslem anxious for the prestige of the Caliph. The movement had two shocks, first when one of its leaders could not produce accounts of the money subscribed, declaring that they would be rendered in heaven, and the cataclysmal one when the Caliph and the Sheikh-ul-Islam were driven from Rum.

Young King Amanullah then a Moslem prodigy, not unnaturally attracted attention. In fact *The Times* correspondent with the preliminary visit of the Simon Commission to India, wrote from Lahore that Kabul was now the spiritual home of Islam in Northern India, and was likely to become the temporal one if ever Hinduism protected in its oppressiveness by British bayonets, ruled at Delhi.

The miserable collapse of the young king, richly deserved in many ways though it was, came as a further shock to Moslems in India, and the throne of Nadir Shah, the restored Durani, is none too secure as yet to be a light to the faithful.

Therefore it is not too much to say, that the Moslem opinion of India is upset, and hardly knows which way to turn. The Islamic faith is unchangeable, and there is little ecclesiastical machinery required. There is no Moslem priesthood ordained to that end. The learned no doubt sit apart, but they cannot rule Islam. In fact this religion has no rulers outside its ordinary government and laws. Any man may lead the faithful at prayer. In India the Government lies in the congregation of each Jama Masjid, the principal mosque of the place. Higher than that there is no hierarchy. The head official of a Jama Masjid is the *Kazi* often an hereditary official, who in countries in which the Government is also Moslem, is the chief Magistrate.

References as to religious order, would if need be, be made to the Sheikh-ul-Islam who from time to time would issue the Caliphs' decision. Without a Caliph and a Sheikh-ul-Islam there is no one to make a *fatwa.* Therefore for the moment Islam is a little forlorn. If a normal course were followed, Islam in India would endeavour to adopt some auto-cephalic system of ecclesiastical government, having a Sheikh-ul-Islam or Sheikh-ul-Hind of its own, as the mouth-piece of an Islamic 'College,' using the term in its widest sense and keeping some such outstanding body as the college of El Azar in Cairo as a final court of religious wisdom.

At the present moment the *Jamiat-ul-Ulema*, with the sanctity of the Moulvis of the Moslem College at Deoband, endeavour to fill the void. Possibly the All-India Moslem Congress and the *Jamiat-ul-Ulema* may evolve an acceptable system.

The Faith of the Prophet has many well-wishers outside its own ranks, who admire the dignity of its precepts and the holiness of its aim. The cry '*La Illa ha, il Allah ho*' has penetrated far beyond its own ranks, shaken the polytheists' temples of Hinduism and earned the reverence of Christianity, as one of the challenges of People of the Book. It is often remarked, however, how little when all is said and done Islam has to offer the introspective soul. However that may be and however Sufism and other sects have tried to fill the void, there have often been those within the fold of orthodoxy, who have far more to teach. Up before the bar of Christianity, Moslem thinkers have tried to teach a closer knowledge of Allah. Wherever mankind has knowledge of a Deity demanding and making for righteousness, there will be room for the thinker who envisages higher service and loftier conceptions as the true meaning of the orthodox belief. In Islam this tendency is often to be seen, especially in modern times, so that here as in Hinduism Moslems shall show a front to the challenge of Christianity, and this factor is an extremely interesting one to watch and understand. Modern Islamic students, however, spend a good deal of time in reading the 'Higher' criticism of the Bible, with the intent, it is true, to belittle its value, but imbibing thereby some application of critical methods to the Qoran and the tenets of Islam.

It has indeed been said that the great feature of modern Islam, is an attack on the New Testament, as a matter of self-preservation. It is this feeling that inspired the Prophet of Qadian in the Punjab, Mirza Ghulam Ahmad, who founded what is known as the Ahmadia sect at the end of the 'eighties of the last century. In contact with missionaries he essayed to teach an Islam that would compete with Christianity in some of the former's hitherto harsher outlooks, and his teaching has many admirable aspects. But he claimed to be the *Mahdi*, and thus aroused hostility, and a Qadiani missionary in Kabul was put to death by Amanullah a few years back. The Qadianis of the modernist section have been responsible for the propaganda of the Woking Mosque Mission, and preach Islam as the religion that the West should adopt.

Among modern Shiahs is the *Bab-i-Bahai*, founded by Mirza Muhammad Ali of Shiraz, who claimed to be the 'Gate of Revelation' for which Shiahs looked.[1] He was executed in 1850, but the Bahai was carried on by Abdul Bahu teaching largely Christian ethics, and in Persia has some 200,000 adherents.

[1] Bab=gate, cf. Bab Illah or Babylon, the Gate of God.

The modern feasts and fasts of Islam are known to most Western folk who travel East. There is the long and very real fast of the Ramazan that lasts the space of a moon, when from sunrise to sunset neither food nor drink passes the lips of the faithful, a real penance, which though legally absolvable in travel, is usually kept even on a long march. After the month of prayer and fasting comes the *Id-ul-Fitr* the Festival of the Breaking. The Muharram is the great Shiah mourning for the death of Hussayn, and his brother Hasan, the grandsons of the Prophet. A model of Hussayn's tomb is carried amid wailing multitudes who in the excitement of their grief often lacerate themselves cruelly, especially in Persia, and formerly in Turkey, instancing to the world once again that there are other things that matter than the things of this world.

Another well-known and popular feasts is the *Bakr-Id* that commemorates the finding of a ram (or goat) in the thicket by Abraham as the substitute for Isaac.

Modern Buddhism

As has been explained in the story of Buddhism told in an earlier chapter, 'Enlightenment' left India many a century ago, the surge of the wilder Moslem tribes through the passes of the north, rooting those few pockets that remained, and destroying the human and architectural beauties of Ghandara. Yet in its various branches it is the religion of 500,000,000 souls in Asia.

It is held in China that all that is best in that country is due to the spread of Buddhism of the High Path, the Path, be it remembered, that taught of divinity and salvation. From China the faith spread to Korea, counteracting the gloom of Taoism and Confucianism, and bringing great centres of peace and meditation. But with the Indian Buddhist missionaries, whose story in itself is a remarkable one, in addition to the teaching of the High Path from Ghandara, came the strange mystical and often erotic teaching of the Mantraya and Tantric Buddhism, which reigns in Tibet to this day. Various schools of thought following this or that ancient teacher still prevail, and Buddhists are sufficiently numerous and active not only to form a very definite body, but to be the one thing that will keep idealism and a way of life before the world of the far East. The school of Nichiren, who taught in the thirteenth century, has many somewhat argumentative adherents, and has been called a 'Protestant' Buddhism. In Korea and Japan flourish the Zen Shu, a school of Meditation, where simplicity and peace are the great features in their shrines and temples, in strong contrast to cathedrals, high dignitaries, and processions of monks that are features of the other branches of 'Enlightenment'. Those in touch with the Buddhism of the Far East and of Southern Asia talk of a considerable revival, as the hope of the lands, the one religion there with a spiritual urge and a really benevolent outlook on the world, and therefore a factor in the world's peace.

The real call to Buddhists apparently, as in both Islam and Hinduism, is the summons to plead their worthiness at the bar of Christianity. Buddhism of the Higher Path desires to show that it too understands a God of Love and Righteousness, and that it knows the secret of mystical communion. The teachings of its mediæval sages in the Far East are being re-studied to this end, while even in the Buddhism of the Low Path as flourishing in Burma, the same teaching of something behind Gautama, is being studied and put forth. A philiosophy, however sublime, cannot for ever take the place of a religion.

A Modern Buddhist Pagoda in Burma

A Modern Hindu Temple in Cawnpore

In Burma and Ceylon as in Siam we have in our midst a flourishing form of Buddhism of the Low Path that meets the daily wants of a contented cheerful people. The curious thing to note however, is that running as an undercurrent in Burma, is the old animism and spirit worship of ancient pre-Buddhist days, and which of course, is existing still in its interesting old ways, among the Mongoloid tribes of the Burmese hills, already referred to. This undercurrent of some old world belief is not unknown in Christian lands, even when nothing remains but the festival worked into Christian routine. It also exists in Siam.

In every village in Burma is the pagoda with the monastery attached, where all the boys are taught and all serve a monk's novitiate. The Buddhist monks, all shaven and shorn, are fed by the people and own no goods, and though it is the custom to speak in advanced circles of the large numbers of saffron-clad monks who live on the community, as the 'Yellow peril', they are very dear to the heart of the people, and the pagodas are the centre of much of the happy rejoicings of the countryside. The monks certainly do teach the youth free of cost, in all that lads should learn in their early days. As women are anathema, and the monks do not touch female education, that branch of modern citizenship is more complicated, but beginning with the Christian schools it is now a subject for the management of the Burmese themselves. The Buddhist thinkers of Burma, as in the Far East, readily recognize that the world owes much to Christianity and are anxious to work with it in uplift and civilization.

In Burmese Buddhism there are no Bodhisatvas, the images some of them of immense size, represent Gautama alone, and do not hold the place of idols, but rather take the place in men's minds as a great reminder that a crucifix does in Catholic countries. The daily service of the temples, the bells that tinkle and pray while men rest, the flags with Pali text that blow in the wind, and are considered as good as a reading, they all have a meaning, a charm, and, let us say, a blessing. The Buddhism of Burma is, it has been said, but a veneer, and it may be so, but it is a veneer that makes for much kindly conduct and right doing. Practical men are content if their religions do even that for the '*oi polloi*', leaving higher conceptions for those who need them and for those who lift up their hands for the others.

The pagodas raise their tall spires as a reminder to those who see them, through the waving bamboos, and hear the daily bells. The services are not largely attended except on festival days, but each morning do the monks and novices drone and chaunt the Pali texts of the *Tripitaka*. The monk, the *Pongyi* which means 'Great Glory', in addition to being fed, is greatly revered, especially by the women he abhors, and all the more so in the Wa season corresponding to the Christian Lent, when the laity bestir themselves in religious ceremony, and which ends in the happy 'Feast of Lanterns'. The New Year's feast comes in April, and is more of a frolic, generally known as the 'Water Feast', but this as some folk say of Christmas Day, is really an old Animistic feast in honour of Thakya Min the Lord of the Nats, for this old world treasures its memories deeply, good or bad.

Mention has been made of the finding of the relics of Gautama in the casket near Peshawur. When these were handed to the Buddhist religious authorities of Burma, a marvellous shrine was built to receive them on Mandalay Hill, which is the outward and visible sign of the Buddhist revival in this country. Famous among those stimulating the revival has been the Ledi Sayadaw, an earnest energetic monk, and among the many good things is the Formation of a Young Men's Buddhist Association (Y.M.B.A.) with, so far as there is a likeness, the same aims towards their young men as the Y.M.C.A. A few Europeans, who have found in Buddhism what they did not know how to look for in their own religion, have taken the yellow robe of the monk, but have not been very highly regarded of the people.

While Buddhism is the national religion of the Burmese in a very definite sense, there are always certain adverse movements, as in other countries. Agnosticism of the young can remain within the Buddhist folds, but it is curious that one of the adverse cults that is definitely hostile, is based on the worship of the *Nats* the old spirit worship and animism referred to. It is admittedly adverse to *Tharanagon*, i.e. religion.

The movements towards higher thought are not so prominent in Burma as in the Far East, the principal body being the Paramats. These include several sects who are adverse to institutional Buddhism and desire the mystical interpretation of the Buddhist scriptures. It is from their ranks that many Christian converts have come, and folk of such mind, are always anxious to accept Christ as a further incarnation of the Divine Spirit in whom they believe.

Lamaistic Buddhism

Allusion has been made to Buddhism in Tibet, and the term applied loosely to Lhassa as the 'Vatican of Buddhism'. That is an attractive expression which is enhanced by the romance of that inaccessible mountain city, and what we now know of its monasteries and nunneries and its holy hill palace and religious centre of the Po-ta-la. But the expression only holds good of the

Buddhism of Tibet, Mongolia, and Manchuria, for whom the Dulai Lama, the ruler of Tibet, is a very real head. The interesting thing about Tibet is that here the power ecclesiastical is also the power temporal, and this dates from when Tsong Kha-pa, the nephew of the first Dulai Lama, in the sixteenth century succeeded in establishing himself as ruler as well as chief priest.

Tibet was first converted from the old pagan 'Bon' to Buddhism in the seventh century by missionaries from India, in the days of King Srong-sau-Gam-pon who had married daughters of the kings of China and Nepal. In the eighth century one Padma Sambara came and introduced magic and many Hindu customs founding also the sect of the 'Red Hats' as the generations rolled on, persecution had almost exterminated the creed. In the tenth century it returned in Mayanistic form, apparently growing very corrupt, until in the fourteenth century a reforming monk, Tsong-Kha, took hold, founding the sect of the 'Yellow Hats', and re-introducing the old monastic life and discipline. In the sixteenth century was founded the office of the Dulai Lama aforesaid. *Lama* more exactly Bla-ma, is a monkish title, and *Dulai* meaning the ocean, though in what sense is not clear, therefore the term Dulai *Lama* means 'Pontiff of the Ocean'. The first Dulai Lama converted Mongolia, and the second as aforesaid established the temporal power. One Lob-Sang-Gyal-Sor, known as the 'Great Fifth', succeeded in uniting Tibet under one control. The Tashi Lama, is a lesser palatine, subordinate to the Dulai Lama. Eventually the Dulai Lama became recognized as the incarnation of a *bodhisatva* who was the original ancestor of the Tibetans, a highly interesting conception. And so it came about that every eighty years or so a Dulai Lama disappears and in his place comes the re-incarnate *Bodhisatva* in the *persona*

MONGOLIAN BUDDHISM
A Chorten or Stupa in Tibet

BUDDHIST ECCLESIASTICS IN LHASA

of a little child, for all the world, like in ribald concept, the birth of the New Year and the shuffling off of the Old, as depicted by Mr. Punch.

Lamaistic Buddhism, like that of China and Japan, is extremely ornate, and conducted with a pomp and ceremony and a wealth of vestments that can vie with the Orthodox or Latin Churches. Great Abbots with their trains appear and disappear and huge processions swell the saints' days. In teaching, the teachings of Buddha as translated years ago by Atisa from Magadha, apparently hold good, in the '*Kanjur-bhak-ngyii*' or 'Translation of Precepts', but it has come by way of Mahayana to be Tantric in many of its manifestations, magic and charms and erotic imagery having come by way of Hinduism. Nevertheless it is in its higher practice a dignified way of life. It is to be seen within British territory of the State of Kashmir in Ladak, where Himis *Lamaserai* is well known to many sportsmen and travellers.

Such as it is, if simpler, is also the Buddhism of the State of Bhutan, within the British umbrella.

Christianity To-day

A very brief outline has been given of the existence of Christianity in India in times far past and of the conversions in Portuguese India, as also of the naturally hesitating attitude of the East India Company in its earlier days, to the propriety of any missionary enterprise. This attitude has always suffered the severest criticism from a purely missionary outlook, using that phrase in a narrow sense. But that attitude was to change as soon as our position in India changed sufficiently for the Government to feel sure of our position. There are very famous names among the Protestant missionaries of the early nineteenth century, who were to take a lead in every good movement in Madras and Bengal. The greatest of the earlier Viceroys, the Marquis Wellesley, had broad enough views, and in twenty years we had the wise and sympathetic *régime* of Lord William Bentinck who gave the missionaries of Serampore his confidence and support, and drew from them much useful advice. Among the names that are for ever famous are Carey, Marshman and Dr. Duff in Bengal already referred to, Schwartz, compelling all men by his character in Madras, Kiernander the Dane aforesaid, Martin the Chaplain, and many another. Their early work is perhaps more famous for the spadework than for the actual conversions, for the sowing rather than the harvest, but such work as the stimulation of higher education and on broad and generous lines, and the placing of Christianity before the intellectual and cultured intellects in Bengal, was by no means the least of their sowings. In the general widening of Britain's horizon, which followed on the Napoleonic happening, missionary societies of all kinds, especially of course the Church Missionary Society, commenced their endeavours, and the Government of India, no longer apprehensive as to the length it might go, removed any prohibition, but wisely and properly had to place restrictions on the active enthusiasm of individual servants. One of the difficulties in early days was the position of converts, whose civic status even the Government was nervous in supporting. With the wave of intelligence taking hold of the world, these troubles vanished, and the missionary work went on very steadily. The harvest was not great, but the individual accessions all over the land among people of the old religions was remarkable in its quiet way. During the sowing, scientific work in India both in the field of practical science, of history, genealogy, forestry, zoology and the like, and in the inside work of ethnological and languistic study, the translation of ancient writings, was largely due to missionary knowledge and zeal. It is the European, and especially the missionary, who has recovered from oblivion all the old knowledge of the Aryan history and literature: and enabled the scientific critics of the world to build up a lost part, and the Indians to restart their old learning. As the Victorian era drew to a close, the fruit of the work in Southern India began to be visible. The harvest suddenly began to ripen, and while the seed that had fallen among well-to-do, and the educated or those whose station in the world of caste is high, was not notable in its harvest, the message went out as did that of early Christianity, to all who were desolate and oppressed. In Southern India during the last quarter of a century the increase of the baptized has been very great. Large Christian communities have grown up, which must now number over five millions. So much is this the case that the term 'mass conversion' and mass movement to Christianity is used, and rightly used. The people who are being converted in large numbers are the 'untouchables' of Southern India, people of whom it was said in 1919 that out of over eight thousand schools in India, only a little over six hundred allowed the 'untouchable' children to enter. Even so recently as 1929 Sir Philip Hartog's interim report to the Simon Commission states the same. Among these people the harvest of years of work is now rushing up from the ground. In two Anglican dioceses the movement is very great, that in Tinevelly and Dornakal; among the other Churches the Press is equally insistent, and from it all comes the great movement for union which will be outlined. The Bishop of Dornakal, the Rt. Rev. V. S. Azariah, is himself an Indian, and leading the movement in his own diocese and in India even as Ramanuja moved, and Gautama taught. The movement among the outcaste and touchable is not confined to Southern India, and is at work in many parts, notably along the frontiers. The uplift in everyday life, in behaviour, in the avoidance of spirit drinking, and the like and the consequent prosperity of the people is remarkable. Hinduism never cared how its Sudras lived and fared, but when a man realizes that Christianity means a special position in this world and the next, and that he is of moral and human importance, then must he act and live accordingly, or so it seems to the Sudra converts. It is but the natural human instinct to be better than the beast, stifled under the contempt of the twice-born. To use the missionary phrase, the 'castemen' watch and those who think approve. In the south, indeed, an appreciable number have become Christians in the last few years. But when a thinking man can have recourse to *Bhakti* teaching, and all the other fine traditions of Hindu reforming sects, or the modern teaching of Islam, the urge of Christianity is not so imperative. All over the land, high caste men do become earnest Christians but the harvest is not yet. On the North-west Frontier, where all are Moslems, it is the medical mission, with its message of mercy among a ruthless folk, that arrests attention, but, again, the harvest is not yet. Exceptions and instances there are many, but among many millions they are trivial, and have no resemblance to what is in progress in the Dravidian lands. In the Punjab itself some remarkable work has been done as related among 'untouchable' and vagrant tribes by the Salvation Army and the Franciscan friars, as well as the Anglican Mission. Prosperous, self-respecting villages have sprung up and crime has disappeared.

The trouble to come may lie in the act that the movement may unavoidably mark the difference between high caste and outcaste, especially now that the untouchables protest so earnestly against Brahmin dominion, and therefore assume a political aspect. That the poor and oppressed should come is so desirable, but that it should unwittingly grow to a movement among Sudras alone will be a tragedy, humanely speaking. That, however, may safely rest with the 'Everlasting Arms,' and man can but endeavour to guide his part of the machine rightly, nowhere better prescribed than in the 'Noble Eightfold Path.'

For many years, however, the tragedy of the Christian 'dispersion' has been evident, not only in India but all over the world's Mission field. The missionary work in India has been actively pressed by the various Free Churches as well as by Anglicans and the Church of Rome. There is room in Eastern sentiment for two great branches of the Catholic Church, but not for a dozen lesser ones. Overlap and mystification was bound to arise. Those baptized into one of the Protestant Churches, who had any education and status, found themselves demanding that the various little Churches, which, through reasons social and political as much as religious, had arisen in the West, once the bonds of allegiance to Rome had been loosed, should not be perpetuated in India. It was absurd, they felt, that Wesleyans, Anglicans, Baptists, Presbyterians, Lutherans, etc., should all be working the same field with different tools. The result has been after several years of an amicable *modus vivendi* that the definite movement for union has become practically a *fait accompli*. Those who are familiar with Church matters know the story well enough as explained to the Lambeth Conference. But in very simple words, by a self-denial and accommodation, which human nature and understanding being what it is has been very real, a united, modified auto-cephalic Episcopal Church will arise in South India which will embrace practically all 'Protestant' bodies using that word to mean Churches not in union with Rome. How the tactic difficulties, religious, human and goodwill of such a union has been overcome and arranged by those leaders in the movement, Bishop Palmer of Bombay, Bishop Whitehead formerly of Madras, and many another, is a fascinating story of itself. Suffice it to say that at any rate in South India there will be generally but two great authorities of Christianity, the Church of Rome and the Episcopal Church of India.

It is not out of place in this connexion to refer to the Anglican Church in India in its ordinary as well as its missionary work. The great Continent, till recently a province of Canterbury but now auto-cephalic, is divided into dioceses. Its normal parish duties, as distinct from what might be called the 'Chaplaincy' of the officers and men of the British Forces, is very largely the educational and congregational care of the large domiciled community, both British born, Indian born and of British or mixed parentage. The number of such is considerable, for whom such matters as diocesan schools, orphanages and the like are by no means trivial. In the cities up-country, the European and Anglo-Indian business community furnish a considerable congregation and need for ministry, chiefly to the Anglican and Roman Church, and in a lesser degree to the Free Churches. The Church of Rome with its dioceses, its convents and its schools, is also spread over the land with plenty to do. Christianity is therefore very much part of the warp and weft of India, while to a continent which has absorbed so many millions of Turks, Tartars and Afghans, there is no question of the British being an alien race. The cathedrals and the churches in the military cantonments, some stately edifices, some otherwise, and the lesser chapels of the smaller communities, stand not unworthily in this country of mosque and temple, as evidences that Christianity is something more than a phrase.

Should the quest for Christianity come suddenly among the caste-folk, as some think it may, in the destruction that modernism threatens to fantastic creeds, there is a reasonably geared machine to receive it, capable of incorporating the immense movement that will be necessary.

Chapter X

THE CONCLUSION OF THE WHOLE MATTER

EAST AND WEST—THE KALEIDOSCOPE—THE RELIGIOUS OUTLOOK —THE PROBLEM OF YOUTH AND EDUCATION—NUMBERS— PALITICS—A VIGNETTE AT DELHI.

East and West

An attempt has been made to pass in review in a very short space four thousand years and all that therein happens, to examine briefly the rise and sometimes the fall of great world religions and to endeavour to estimate, their position in the world. This has been done but to one end, the familiarizing of the ordinary reading public of the Empire who had all too little time to search with this great problem that is India. And when it has all been done there can be but one question. "Watchman what of the night?" Seeing all that India is at the present moment, those who know their Mr. Jorrocks might be inclined to say with that famous character, as he opened the cupboard door in mistake for the window, "plaguey dark, and smells of cheese." Is it plaguey dark? That is the real question. I have ventured to quote more than once from Sir Alfred Lyall, because I have always found more understanding in his work than in everything else that has been said. Among his many searching verses he wrote *Ex Occidente Vox*, and he also wrote the reply. It is too long to give *in extenso*, but the opening of the quest traces the great task in which the warp and weft of fate have drawn the British race bidding them pick up and re-cement the thousand pieces into which the great Tartar Empire of Delhi broke, when it fell from its pedestal, a Tartar empire that did but fulfil the weird of Kanishka. And this is how he begins, . . . 'Britania loquitur,'

"Many a year have my sons gone forth
Their bones are bleaching in field and flood
They have carried my name from the Ancient North
They have borne it high through water and blood."

That is the opening, fitting enough, when we think of the countless little European cemeteries in India, north, south, east and west, in which every man, every woman and every child who die there, have passed before their time in the service of India which Rudyard Kipling has called the 'grim step-mother of our kind'.

West says to East in the promise of peace to develop:

"Some arms deep rusted, an old world rhyme
A broken idol a ruined fane
May linger as waifs of the wild foretime
When the Gods were cruel and the men were slain.

"Let the Temple moulder in gathering shade
Let the stones lie strewn in the cedar grove
Ye shall rule like gods in a glorious land
Ye shall live by knowledge and peace and love."

To West, East then speaks:

"O men of the wandering sea borne race
Your venture was high but your wars are done
Ye have rent my veil ye behold my face
What is the land that your arms have won."

But the East, fatalist at heart, ends:

"The burden of thought and the travail of care
Weigh down the soul in its wandering flight
The sun burns ever the plains lie bare
It is death brings shade and the dreamless night."

These lines in their simple rhythm sum up in uncertain line and certain goodwill the whole problem.

The Kaleidoscope

Looking as we have done on the countless intermingled pieces, of many colours, of many races and of bitterly different mentalities no-one can fail to marvel at all that the nineteenth century has brought forth. Escape from internecine wars, a ceasing of that riding forth of vast masses of predatory horse from their haunts in the Nerbudda jungles, complete freedom to all classes and races, some attention to the humanities and amenities of man and beast—the rivers spread over the face of desert lands to the watering of millions of acres, thousands of miles of railways, universities innumerable, truly a great site prepared for the building. The more we see of the countless jarring and conflicting interests, the intense proclivities of certain classes to evil and outlawry, the underground workings for evil, partly for gain and partly from hate, the vast scale on which disasters and happenings may come to pass, the more must we wonder at the patience of those who have restored the edifice.

Assuming that our sympathies are wholly with, let us say, the Hindu who would wish that his ancient race and ancient faith should justify itself religiously and politically, or that we wish that mighty Islam in India should feel free of any disability, let us turn over in our minds what could be done. Immediately are we up against certain facts. There is no Moslem province that is not equally largely a Hindu one, there is no Hindu *régime* that is not honeycombed with larger numbers of untouchable classes who hate them bitterly and who can only be kept in Hindu bounds by cruelty. If we turn to a Moslem state, such as that ruled over by the premier prince in India, the descendant of the mighty Asaf Jah Mogul, we find that his people other than the comparatively few thousands who have hied to his city and protection, are Hindu. Do we turn to some Hindu prince we find him ruling aboriginals, Moslems, and others who outnumber those of his own faith. In Kashmir, where the rule is Hindu, the people are Moslem groaning often under punishment for such crimes as eating a piece of beef. Where an Indian prince would rule happily, avoiding in the old days rebellion, and to-day dissatisfaction which will bring him into disrepute with the British Government, he has to tread very wisely and warily. Would Hindu reformers, as the clever university debater urges, set forth to carry academical reforms of faiths and customs, go back to the old or come away from it with a high hand, an outcry would set up that would re-echo from Peshawur to Cape Cormorin. Intensive Hindu reform with British bayonets to suppress the objectors is hardly thinkable.

Lord Curzon's partition of Bengal was a statesman-like attempt to create a Moslem province that should be a home of Islamic development, and a Hindu one that should let Hinduism work out its salvation and Bengal would have none of it. *Festina lente*, make haste very slowly, frequent neither high path nor low, has been the only way of safety.

The Religious Outlook

So much has been said of the conflict of religions that it is tempting to try and guess how things can possibly trend. We have seen the tenets of the Arya Samaj making great progress, and appealing to a spirit that blends religion with nationalism so far as that may be possible on religious lines. We have also seen how theosophy attracts whose whom modern education has left rudderless. But in studying the race-proud age-old Brahminism steeped in the pride of race and re-incarnation we see there can be no turn towards Christianity by the twice-born, that human agency can assist. Equally can we believe that Islam born of the desert, fostered by the sword, and finding its strength in its unbending monotheism, has no early use for a creed so like its own as Christianity. To the inquirer with whom the world is going well, Christianity is not likely to appear intensely desirable. Twice-born Hindu and righteous Moslem may thank their Gods that they are not as other men are. It is to the poor and lowly, and all that are desolate and oppressed, in mind, body and estate, that there comes the uplift of the Christian missionary and its great appeal and comforter. For the others the agency can not be in man's hands.

That is what now the missionary understands, and as has been said, prefers to see how far he and the faiths around him can keep in step to promote a more righteous world, leaving time and Providence to do the rest.

A dream that young men may dream, and the vision that old men may see, is a Hinduism urged by some teacher that can persuade his own people of his orthodoxy . . . whether some follower of Dayanand, or some one going back to Ramanuja, some teacher with the power and will

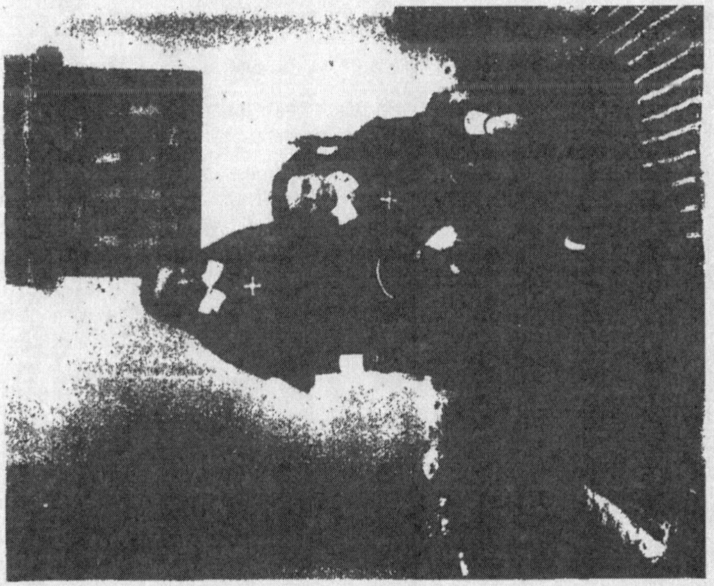

and magnetism to bring popular Hindus from its evil ways and devil-born excrescences . . . an Islam in India content and with some auto-cephalic organization that can close its ranks in the cause of humanity and good will, and make its power of full avail. . . . Christianity spreading among the Dravidians of the south and driving forth the devils that make men afraid, or embracing the humble folk up country, while waiting in the north for those, Hindu or Moslem, who may be ready to come to it. The rest must remain with the centuries.

There is room for some great congress of the leaders of religion in India in the interest of goodwill, and of at least education, on better lines than theosophy can offer, and there is a haunting fear that faces all, Christian and Moslem, Parsee and Sikh, and must bring them all together. That is the trouble, the bitter disappointed agnosticism, that is coming over the good lads when they leave their simple homes, not only for the Universities of India, but for the schools and colleges of Britain.

The Problem of Youth and Education

It is to be remembered that India is now a country of great Universities, some Hindu, some Moslem, mostly mixed, but on the British model, in which British and Indian teachers turn out a number of undergraduates, more indeed unfortunately than the needs of the East at present can find careers for. They are like all townsfolk of India almost entirely divorced from the country life which is the real India. But the level of the Universities is high, and arts and science as there taught is turning out men of world fame. Unfortunately below it the school systems of India do not yet provide that character building fabric which is so great a necessity, and which should go with higher education. Here and there Mission schools have taken a wonderful lead, and their services have been much sought after for lads of all faiths. The multitude of religious aspects places some difficulty in imparting religious training as the great basis and hold-fast of life. In all universities students love to let their dreams and fancy wander up and down the realm of both worlds. In India, unless perhaps from a Hindu family where *Bhakti* is taught, the young men of to-day have no great anchor. In the universities it will be found that youth, Hindu, Sikh and even Moslem, scoffs at all religion. Here in Britain where so many come, and where however complete club and hostel arrangements may be, the divorce from the rule of life of their family is naturally and unavoidably greater, it is but to be expected that religious divorce should be even greater. The lads openly scoff, and do not see enough of the more edifying side of Christian life to help them. A vast agnostic class is growing up among the intelligentzia, that is a great danger to all, and both Hindu and Moslem may well be anxious. Islam can be presented sufficiently clearly to appeal to reason, but with all the flummery of popular Hinduism, the case for the young Hindus is different. When half-gods go, it is not easy to replace them, and the Arya Samaj is perhaps the only outlook for intelligent Hindus to crawl to safety in. In this connection it is well to know of the Christa Siva Sangha, a movement that is being developed in Southern and Western India under the magnetic personality of Father Winslow. The endeavour is to follow the ancient way of the *ashram*, to copy the way of the *acharya*, and to bring friendliness and assistance to students and the young intelligentzia, by living in a community and a fraternity. The difficulty is for the young enthusiast from Home to be put through a sufficiently informing course of all that the British in India stand for, to give him sufficient judgement to help student life, and abstain from the baby abuse that swells so much in student circles. The movement has astounding possibilities and may even put a stop to the *bomb-parast* cult, but it has difficulties that need fathering.

In this matter of youth and education, the Interim Report of the Simon Commission dealing with Education, and compiled by Sir Philip Hartog, is of extraordinary interest.

It is worth alluding to the manner in which the British staffs in schools and Universities have succeeded in introducing British games into their institutions. For many years has cricket flourished with football and hockey, and Eastern lads have taken to them very heartily—yet it cannot be said they have yet had the success in the general formation of character looked for. During the World War, young Bengal insisted on raising a battalion for Mesopotamia, lads running away from school in their zeal. It had a wonderfully good football team, but was of no use as a military weapon, despite great attempts to assist it. Nevertheless amongst its Indian (Bengali) officers were one or two brilliant exceptions. This race as a whole, despite its game prowess, had no proclivity for military service. In the difficult work of flying, when the energy and courage is more mental than physical, success may be considerable.

Numbers

The matter of numbers is always important, especially to those whose horizon is limited by the British Isles and those who think the millions of Greater London a serious proposition. The figures, where given in this book, are based on the census of 1921. Those of the census just taken show an increase from 316,000,000 to 350,000,000 possibly in part due to better enumeration, but also an evidence of Eastern fecundity . . . an increase of over 10 per cent. The details are not yet out, but anyone wishing to have more up-to-date figures may safely assume a normal increase all round, and add 10 per cent., with the exception that there is probably a much higher figure necessary for Christian denominations, where increase does not depend on birth-rate.

The denominational figures are as follows, for the whole of India of which perhaps 25 per cent. are in the Indian states, which actually comprise two-fifths of India in area.

Under the heading of Indo-Aryan religions 232,773,000 viz.:

Hindu	216,261,000
Aryas	468,000
Brahmos	6,000
Sikhs	3,239,000
Jain	1,178,000
Buddhist (chiefly Burma)	11,571,000
Parsee	102,000

Under the heading Semitic:

Moslems	68,754,000
Christians	4,754,000 (6,000,000 in 1930)
Jews	22,000

Under the heading Primitives:

Animists	9,775,000
Unclassable	18,000

Even at the risk of persistence it is necessary to emphasise on paper again the great extent of India, as large as Europe, less Russia, and as populous. France, Germany, Austria, Italy, the Netherlands, Spain, etc., etc., all in one . . . but whereas these latter are all in one main religion and all act to the instinctive control of Decalogue, in India are all the religions and races referred to with countless other mainsprings and reactions. Then again there are over seven hundred Princes' States[1] in alliance with the British Crown and not with an Indian Parliament, and extremely cognizant of the fact.[2]

That, by the light of numbers, is the complex which the British with the tacit support of and active assistance of the bulk of the people, have rescued from a chaos far worse than that into which China has fallen. It is enough to show the task, to emphasize the astounding success, and to see how difficult is any new orientation that is not developed gradually, and of great wisdom. And with it all is that right which the prompters of this good enterprise have, in business metaphor, to their share of the profits in perpetuity.

PALITICS

There is a quaint Irish story, which is perhaps germane at this stage. A young Irishman went into the confessional in some distress. "Father," he said, "I've a terrible thing on my mind. I hardly dare tell you." "My son," replied the father, "tell your priest and Mother

[1] They vary in size from half that of France to that of Battersea Park.

[2] An interesting point is the figures of Islam as a whole, estimated only in countries where a census is not possible or taken. Europe 18 million, Africa 60, Asia 157. 94 million of whom 70 are Indian in the British Empire. 39 in the Netherlands Empire. France 32. Various 23. Under Moslem rule 47 million. Under Western rule 188.

Church, for it's your duty." "Father, father, I've shot a policeman." And a stern voice came back. "Pat! How often have I told you that I will not have palitics in the Confessional."

But in looking out to the future, it is almost impossible to think of a religious future without some reference to the political one, in this strange, re-riveted continent, whose ultimate faiths are so diverse and antipathetic, and which every one in Britain wants to see progress and be prosperous. One can imagine the genuine Hindu reformers, the Brahmo or the Arya Samajist, longing for a Hindu Power, and an organised hierarchy which could compel acceptance of reform by a strong arm and a compelling education. But those who have any historical sense know how hard it is for reforms to come this way. Even a Mussolini, with his disciplined eager hearts behind him, knows well enough where his boundary lies. But even if under certain conditions such a thing were possible elsewhere, the interwoven conditions would render it out of the question in India. It is of course true that Great Britain has discouraged its governments in India from pressing on any reforms that clash with religious customs. As guardian and picker up of pieces the support of the people has always been the most important of all considerations. Only those decayed customs which drew the horror of the civilized world, the burning of widows, the destruction of female children and the like have been restrained. The rest, the general uplift was to come through the restoration of law and order, the development of education, the spread of every sort of science and the training of Indians therein. These were all to bring as they have done a hundredfold, results in their gain, and it is as expected that the rest could and would be done by the people themselves.

It was in pursuit of such a policy of development with the support of all concerned, that the Montford Reforms were brought in, in succession to the sensible ones of Lord Morley, as part of our general promise to India and as the goal of that astounding development which has never been better told than in Part 1 of the Simon Report. That those reforms were hurried on by lesser men when Great Britain was in the throes of finishing the War and when her greater men were too weary to think hard, is one of ours and India's misfortunes. It fell to the lesser men to work in a hurry, and now that the veil has been partly lifted by the publication of Mr. Edwin Montagu's Diaries, it is possible to see that the foundations needed more thought. Nevertheless Great Britain deserved every sort of enthusiastic support in her endeavours, and did not get it. The British instinct is always a generous one, and throwing itself, as did the nation and the British officials in India, into the spirit of the Reforms, it had a right to expect a better attitude from the politically minded folk of Bengal and the intelligentzia generally. Such a support, in reality, would have been the height of Machiavellian policy, for it would have produced such a feeling in Britain, that this country would have stripped it itself in its enthusiasms and renunciation.

The intelligentzia of India especially of south and west are in a different category from those of any other contemporary country, owing to the strange way in which Eastern Aryanism has developed. Never has their hand kept their head. Never have they been able to withstand hardier and braver races, with the result that ever since Mahmud of Ghuzni crossed the Indus have they been in a suppressed state, waiting in suppression with all the consciousness of their twice born origin and the *karma* that controls them. Not from them came soldiers for the World-War.

Even in the days of the Hindus kings who tore up in internecine strife the empires of Asoka, of Harsha and the like, it is not they who have wielded the Aryan sword. Brains galore to direct the sword in other men's hands, skill to handle finance, grey matter to chop logic, but never the heart to stand in the breach themselves. Here in Britain, however much we respect law and order brains and mental attainments, every man is believed to have the capacity to play the man if need be. Were this quality suspect, there is little enough of reverence that the other qualities would receive. Nevertheless it is so assumed that we do not find it necessary to search for it. With a physical timidity goes the failure often enough to follow right and duty in the face of threatened violence, a failing that India suffers from very much.

So great is the want of physical courage, as understood in the west, the case, that out of the three hundred and fifty millions of India it has been estimated that ten millions alone can find men of physique and the necessary courage to serve as soldiers. The difference between one soldier of the northern races and a thousand of the southern men is beyond belief to those who have seen it not. The qualities of brain and endeavour that may be, nay undoubtedly do lie, in these southern brains are great and many. When they left their ancient uplands, something left them too. Thousands of years of heat and Hinduism gone wrong, have done evil that a generation cannot mend. That this is so is evidenced by the contempt of the northern races. The idea that the sons of many of the intelligentzia of this type, can take their places besides the sturdy yeomanry and gentry of the Punjab as officers, seems to the British officer in India a ludicrous conception. Those who clamour for their sons to hold such positions have little knowledge of what is required. To the man of little physique and no physical courage the grip of fear, that paralysing failure of mind and limbs to act, is rarely experienced by him under the kindly British umbrella, that covers him. It lies dormant till the occasion arises. The man who grovels before the dacoit and knows that he is "a very fearsome man", is not the one who tries to handle Indian politics. Never for a thousand years has anything Indian been able to prevent the invasion and conquest of India, and it was not till the thin red line to whom even the Kaiser was a joke and a jest, reached the Indus and trained the yeomen of the north to stand beside it, that the inroads to India ceased. These are points that cannot be overlooked, and indeed the Simon Report, does not overlook it. The Indian politician who so often suffers from that most terrible of maladies, the 'inferiority complex', feigns to forget all the hard facts of his past.

Or, alternately if he does remember them, he casts them up as the result of the machinations of the impure British Government, something in this wise.[1]

Am I an hereditary coward who any man may kick? It is your fault.

Is my cowardice the result of countless years of child wives and immature fathers? It is your fault.

Are the Indian villagers of poor physique, because in a thousand years no one has stopped them leaving the burrows whence their villages are built, as mosquito haunts? It is your fault.

Am I so inextricably bound to my family that I cannot but serve their interests even when I am in authority, before all others? It is your fault.

Am I hopelessly inclined to oppress and rob all unfortunates put into my power? It is your fault.

[1] *Vide* Mr. Ghandi, *The Times*, July 3, 1930.

And so forth, the theory being that a century and a half of British control and stimulation has so dimmed a sense of responsibility that all these evils, evils in reality of thousands of years of Hinduism, have arisen from it. Where—as every move forward and every good thing is the result of British attempts to bring very backward folk forward, but to rule them as Eastern folk and not as Western. It might be possible to say that the evils were due to the years of Moslem domination, Turk and Tartar and Afghan but even then, history says that the evil which admitted of such invaders and conquerors is far older still.

It would be well to slurr over these points, were it not right that British folk should know something of what their countrymen have had both with and against them, and may to some extent arm them against the super-sentimentalism that is so easily stirred in England. For over a century has Great Britian sent the pick of her schools and colleges to work in this great land, many, alas, to leave their bones prematurely in its often neglected cemeteries.

One more point is worthy of some consideration. For close on half a century, there has been in unofficial existence the National Congress, a self-organized and self-constituted body with no particular functions, that has tried to resemble an Indian parliament. Great persistence and much talking has taken place over the years that the congress has eaten. It is a problem whether the failure to 'rope' this body into the great work of the re-building, that year by year has grown more complete, was avoidable, or whether the soul implacability, which has grown under the heel of the Moslem conquerors, has made it quite impossible as a coadjutator or one that could be co-opted. Possibly the knowledge that the millions of the best of India were heart and soul with the Government, has made it all these years careless of the 'sourity'. For ten years and more has Viceroy after Viceroy called on Mr. Ghandi to 'come let us reason together', to help at the wheel of progress, to save the girl wives, to rescue the outcast from their outlawry, and generally to bear a hand in the work, to lead an advanced political wing, to do anything useful and helpful and human. But *Baba* Ghandi has always cried 'unclean—unclean!' even while a kindly British surgeon removed his inflamed unclean appendix to save his life. To spin *kadr* cloth, to wear *kadr* clothes, to abuse all Western progress, to ride in trains and motor cars, and live by grace of the British scalpel, is also typical of the land where the robin wears a red back behind, instead of a red breast before. But the *Baba* has preferred to tread a road that has led to more than one Cawnpore, and more than one holocaust of hysteria. It is all bad enough and a thought and a sight to make angels weep. Then while the world wonders and the unsentimental French who run their Eastern and African empires with a strong hand, scoff, there comes the voice of the prophetess, Helen Mayo, to show them something of the impasse into which the stress of many religions, and the tyranny of Hinduism gone sour, had brought the land that once plumped for 'Enlightenment'.

Behind, however, the political clamour, and the inferiority complexes, lies this astounding search of the people of India for 'release', for the something whatever it is that lies behind the universe. By way of the Atman and Enlightenment, by way of tortures and *tapas*, by ways of the prophet and the sacred fire, the search for the 'jewel' within the lotus' has continued through the ages. When they shall find it and how, is in God's hands and not ours to say. Whether Britain shall be worthy to lead India across the Jordan or whether another, nobody in this world can say, but Great Britain, on the balance of good and evil and before the bar of the world, need not fear verdict of her past history in this matter, in their attempt to sweep a path for the way. But the patent truth is fairly well accepted in the world, and nowhere more than in the real India, that Great Britain with an over-riding authority can alone help those 350,000,000 along any sort of way. The building of a condominium which shall ensure this, while giving full scope to all that is good and great in India, and will secure due tribute to the countless British dead in India's service, and due recognition to the many million pounds sent to India, is in reality no very difficulty matter, if heads remain sane. The simple side of this continent of people, of whom nine-tenths and more are cultivators, for whom the British magistrate alone cares, is perhaps illustrated by this story of Mr. Hickson, the faithhealer at Delhi, as the writer saw it, and which perhaps strikes a note on which this book may close:

> "The ploughman settles the share
> More deep in the grudging clod
> For the Earth, the wheat is my care
> And the rest is the will of God."—Kipling.

A Vignette at Delhi

> "For the gods who have mercy, who save or bless
> Are the vision of man in his helplessness."—Lyall.

It was my good fortune to strike something of the pilgrim spirit in another guise a few years ago, when Mr.

Hickson came to Delhi, during his mission to India, and a very remarkable sight it was.

Riding through the battered Kashmir Gate one morning at Delhi I found a vast Indian crowd surging round the English church of Byzantine form, that Colonel James Skinner had built many a year before. The Kashmir Gate itself, crumbling and shell beaten, the breach up which John Nicholson had led the stormers in '57, the beautiful old church with the gold cross and dome riddled by shell splinters. What a setting for a healing missioner!

Outside the sweep of a battered wall, inside the monuments to those who had fallen to the wild fury of the mob and the mutineer, pathetic in memory, eloquent of the avenger. But the stones of Delhi cry aloud of far greater tragedy and drama than even '57, of Nadir Shah, the Persian Turk, who massacred the populace as a warning, piling high their heads by the wayside: of the last of the Moguls blinded by his minister and of the later day, when Farmer George reigned in England, when all Maratha chivalry went down before Afghan lance and knife, where now green lawns and white railings portend peace. Then why on that autumn morning in the year of our Lord 1921, being 1299 of the Hejira in the kalendar of Islam, did the people struggle and press round the church of old James Skinner, 'Old *Sekunder*' as folks loved to call him.

So wondering, I pulled my horse aside and after the manner of the English, I asked a policeman. Why should prince and pauper crowd to a Christian church? The roads fluttered bunting in preparation for a Royal visit, but that was still ahead. Why press the maim and the halt, *Sahib* and the *sais*, the Christian and the Hindu, the *Mem* and the Moslem? The princes and the kings had not yet come, nor the legions, rank on rank. The answer I got from the young Punjabi policeman was an amazing one. 'God was performing miracles in the church' . . . No, he had not seen himself, but this one knoweth and that one saith . . . he was a constable, and his business was to keep the crowd from pressing . . . "Steady, brothers. Keep back there! See the Inspector *Sahib* cometh."

"But why," I persisted, "do the Muhammadans and Hindus, nay and Parsees too . . . press into the *Sahibs'* church " How was he to know? He was a constable, and all crowds were the children of Satan . . . of a surety all the world, as the *Sahib* knows, looks for a portent, a helper. The sun burns ever, the plains lie bare . . . man is ever in need of God be he Hindu or Moslem . . . and folks this week past have been flocking to this *Sahibs'* church, and the *padre* . . . no, not the usual *padre* . . . a new *padre* with a wonderful voice, had come from none knew where, and prayed all the morning, and put his hands on the sick . . . see the litters even now coming up! There is old mother Allah Vissayah paralysed these six years. See! her grandsons bear her . . . she has been thrice and already they say she walks."

And I rode on, my *sais*, eagerly asking if he too might go to church. Could it be true? Was Jesus of Nazareth passing, Jesus the *Nazara, Isa ibn Miriam!* [1]

Of a truth the crowd said yes, for on the grass outside the porch lay litter by litter, dandy and doolie and native bed, those that could not walk to the pool, that altar in the church of the English, where the deep-voiced Englishman prayed and touched. Inside the people stood and sat rank on rank . . . all the creeds waiting the keys

[1] Jesus, the Son of Miriam.

thereof . . . and through the stained glass window poured the morning sun of the East, the crown of thorns fretted on the marble floor, the purple robes of a Roman soldier throwing a light on the slab to the British centurion who rested below.

And then the organ swelled and prayer gave place to hymn, while the stream of sick to the altar flowed steadily and passed out comforted, the aged Hindu leading his crumpled wife, Moslem and Fire-worshipper and Indian Christian. Small ailing children in arms clutched the ticket that told of their disease, infants chewed theirs, while mothers waited patiently, and all the while outside the constable shouted, "Peace, brothers, peace! There is time for all things . . . press not on the gates, but wait the *Hukm*."[1]

And thus they told me for seven days the crowd had been pressing and all the city side spoke of the marvels. It was a strange revelation of psychology, these races flocking to the church of the strangers at some call, some rumour that help was at hand for humans . . . and the soldiers from the world's end had heard the message, the pensioners, the battered drafts of years gone by, the men of Egypt, of Mesoptamia, and of Flanders, pressed for their share of the tidings.

There were Christians too among the crowd and in the Church, Christians of all degrees, some who had come from curiosity, others who would fain go inside but lacked, perhaps, the courage, or shirked the publicity, to demand healing of God whom they had so long neglected, feeling perhaps too, as Naaman felt, chagrined that they were asked to bathe in this simple Jordan rather than in Abana and Pharpar.

And it was thus that the message came to Delhi, while

[1] Order.

the city was waiting to receive the great Prince and his mission from the King. It reflected too a demand that Mr. Ghandi and his followers urged, that the world should be ruled by kindness alone, that impracticable demand in this hardhearted universe.

Behind the flummery of popular Hinduism and its crimson stones, behind the fanatics of every day Islam, lies a great simplicity of belief. God is in Heaven, and all can be well with the world, which is at the opposite pole to that Hinduism which deals with the organs of birth and the circlet of bones, and the loose loves carved on the temple stones. It was this subconscious belief in a world-mercy, and the human desire for a portent, that brought the creeds of the East flocking to the church of 'Old Sekunder'.

And all the while the army was pouring in by road and rail for the function, and delegates and councillors were making their mark, and the telegraph was clicking news of the gatherings of troops and of princes. The heavy trains ran in through the bastions of the Selimghar and squadrons and batteries jingled down the roads, and even the cannon roared out salutes to princely power and place.

The jolly country folk were coming in to market, father, mother and children. The camel vans were full of travellers lumbering over the country roads, the beautiful domes of the great mosque shone in the morning sun and the mullahs called the faithful to prayer. It was just an every day morning, neither prayer nor fast day, but the country folk and the beggars were coming to town and folk were getting ready for the merry making. Over the Jumna bridge jogged conjurer and juggler, monkeys and bears, pimp and pander, faqirs and free lances, saints and sinners, while the Hindu ascetics in the shrines tell their beads.

POPULAR HINDUISM
Procession of Ascetics at the great Hindu Fair at Allahabad

They had seen it all before. Ever since time was had kings and emperors ridden to Delhi, 'And the cannons roar and the bayonets gleam.'

"Here as I sit by the Jumna bank
Watching the flow of the sacred stream,
Pass me the legions rank on rank."

"Is it a god or a king that comes,
Both are evil and both are strong,
With women and worship and dancing and song
Carry your god and your kings along."

To have seen it all before, ever since the beginning of time, and to know that it is chalk on granite, to sit unmoved, seeking only peace on a road untold. Thus it is that the true Hindu ascetic sits, oblivious of the pomp and vanity of the press in the city or the anxious crowd in the churchyard hardby, but personal in his religion, recks little of the cry for help that goes heavenward, as Hindu and Moslem look for a portent and cry for help. Does the portent truly lie up by the bastion of the Kashmir Gate, amid the memories of old James Skinner, whom men called *Sekunder* the Fortunate? It seemed so.

Then out from the crowded nave, passed the processions to the altar. I slowly pressed my way and came again to the policeman at the gate. I asked if he found the crowd still masterful. He did not. Why should he? Was he not a constable of the great *Sirkar*, and miracle or no miracle, he had but to order and they to obey. Yes, it was true that some crowds were the real children of Satan, but not this one. No! A young *padre Sahib* had come outside and said, 'Wait, the healer will come out to you,' and the people had become quiet. Besides, he also had told them it was an order. See!

And I looked and the crowd pressed again. The healer had come out into the cool churchyard and was busy among the litters and it seemed as if the message was the same as in the days long past—

ὕπαγε ἡ πίστις σου σέσωκέ σε [1]

[1] Arise, thy faith hath saved thee. (BLIND BARTEMEUS.)

SHORT GLOSSARY OF WORDS IN COMMON USE IN CONNECTION WITH EASTERN RELIGIONS

Atman. The soul.

Bairagi. A Hindu ascetic.
Bhagwan or Bhagavan. God.
Bhagavad-gita. Song of adoration. A famous Hindu book of praise.
Bhakti. The Hindu salvation cult.
Brahm. The supreme power behind the universe.
Brahma, or Brahman. The First Person of the Hindu Trinity.
Brahmin. The sacred priestly class among Aryans.
Bikshu. A religious beggar.

Churel. Ghost of a woman dead in childbirth.

Dussera. Hindu Festival of Spring.
Dewali. Hindu 'Harvest Home' Festival.
Deva. A godlet.
Dharma. Religion (Hindu).
Din. Religion (Muhammadan).
Eed. v. Id.

Faqir. Muhammadan religiou mendicant.

Gosain. Hindu mendicant under vows.
Guru. Religious teacher.
Granth. The Sikh Scriptures.

Id. Religious Festival (Muhammadan).
Ishvara. The supreme Deity (Hindu).
Islam, The Muhammadan religion and communion.

Jogi. v. Yogi. (Popular form of Yogi).

Karma. The deeds of a man's life.
Krishna. The popular Hindu hero and teacher. Later declared to be an incarnation of Vishnu.

Linga. The male organ of generation, especially of the God Siva.

Mahayuga. The great cycle of the worlds existence.
Mahabharata. A famous Hindu epic, and law giving.
Manu. A Hindu lawgiver.
Mantra. An incantation hymn.
Moulvi. A Muhammadan religious teacher.
Mulla. A Muhammadan scripture reader.
Muharram. Muhammadan festival of mourning.
Moslem. A follower of Islam, a Muhammadan.
Mussalman. Another form of 'Moslem'.
Muslim. Another spelling of 'Moslem'.

Nirvana or Nibbana. The state of heavenly rest that is to end the period of incarnations.

Pali. The language in which the Buddhist Canon is preserved.
Prakit. Old Aryan vernaculars.
Puranas. Hindu semi-religious songs concerning ancient matters.
Paryrajakas. Religious wanderers.

Prajapati. Early Aryan name for God.
Pithi. Female generative organ in religious imagery.
Puja. Worship.

Qoran. The Sacred Scripture of Islam.

Rama. A popular Hindu legendary, identified as an incarnation of Vishnu.
Ramayana. The great epic retailing the adventures and precepts of Rama.
Ramazan. The Moslem month of fasting.
Rishi. A Seer.

Sati. A widow burning. A widow who devotes herself on her husbands pyre. (= good).
Sadhu. A religious ascetic.
Sannyassin. A recluse.
Siva. *v*. Vishnu
Sufi. Moslem mystic fraternity.
Swami. The usual term for a hermit meaning 'Lord'.
Sanskrit. The old literary Aryan tongue as appose to Prakrit, the vernaculars.
Shiah. The branch of Islam that recognises only the family of the Prophet as Caliph.
Sruti. The Hindu Canon.
Smirti. The Hindu tradition.
Sutra. Hindu hymn.
Sutta. Buddhist hymn.
Sura. The chapters of the Qoran.
Stupa. A monument to the Buddha.
Sunni. Moslem Orthodoxy.
Samaj. A society.

Tapas. Religious Austerity, or Rule of Life.

Upanishads. Joyous Hymns of Praise and Adoration of God. (Hindu).

Vedas. The Early Hindu Scriptures.
Vishnu. One of the two great names under which Hindus worship the Almighty.

Yoni. The female organ of generation, used in Hindu imagery with the Linga.
Yoga. A System of Philosophy and Mysticism (Hindu).
Yuga. An age or cycle.
Yogi. One who practises Yoga.

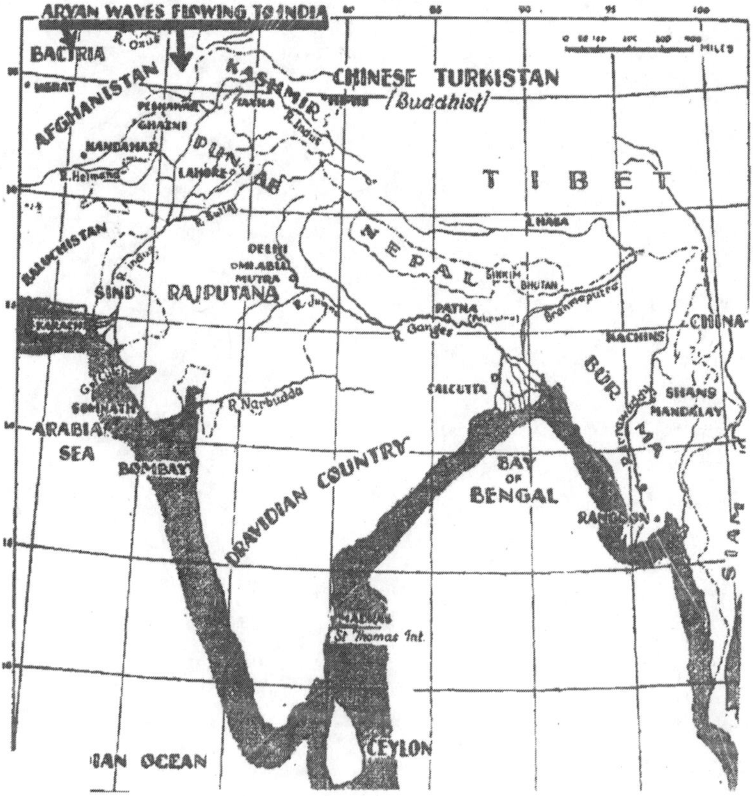

OUTLINE of INDIA
In days Ancient & Modern

1. Moslems predominate in the Punjab, but-
2. Sikhs about Lahore
3. Animists where ever there are wild hills & forests.
4. The valleys of the Ganges & Jumna are the real Aryan centre.
5. Hindus & Untouchables are

INDEX

T

U

W

X